The Ultimate Indoor Games Book

The Ultimate Indoor Games Book
The 200 Best Boredom Busters Ever!

Veronika Alice Gunter

LARK BOOKS
A Division of Sterling Publishing Co., Inc.
New York

Art Director: Tom Metcalf
Creative Director: Celia Naranjo
Illustrator: Clay Meyer
Art Assistant: Bradley Norris
Editorial Assistance: Delores Gosnell

Library of Congress Cataloging-in-Publication Data

Gunter, Veronika Alice.
  The ultimate indoor games book : the 200 best boredom busters ever! /
Veronika Alice Gunter.— 1st ed.
    p. cm.
  Includes index.
  ISBN 1-57990-625-7 (hardcover)
  1. Indoor games. I. Title.
GV1229.G86 2005
793—dc22

                              2005006054

10 9 8 7 6 5 4 3 2 1

First Edition

Published by Lark Books, A Division of
Sterling Publishing Co., Inc.
387 Park Avenue South, New York, N.Y. 10016

Text © 2005, Lark Books
Illustrations © 2005, Clay Meyer

Distributed in Canada by Sterling Publishing,
c/o Canadian Manda Group, 165 Dufferin Street
Toronto, Ontario, Canada M6K 3H6

Distributed in the U.K. by Guild of Master Craftsman Publications Ltd., Castle Place, 166 High Street, Lewes, East Sussex, England BN7 1XU
Tel: (+ 44) 1273 477374, Fax: (+ 44) 1273 478606, e-mail: pubs@thegmcgroup.com, Web: www.gmcpublications.com

Distributed in Australia by Capricorn Link (Australia) Pty Ltd., P.O. Box 704, Windsor, NSW 2756 Australia

If you have questions or comments
about this book, please contact:
Lark Books
67 Broadway
Asheville, NC 28801
(828) 253-0467

Manufactured in China

ISBN 1-57990-625-7

For information about custom editions, special sales, premium and
corporate purchases, please contact Sterling Special Sales Department
at 800-805-5489 or specialsales@sterlingpub.com.

Contents

Why Play?

All work and no play makes Jack a dull boy.

All work and no play makes Jack a dull boy.

All work and no play makes Jack a dull boy.

All work and no play makes Jack a dull boy.

All work and no play makes Jack a dull boy.

Go without play for too long, and your body and brain grow sluggish. You get boring.

Play even just a little, and you get creative. As in more interesting. More fun to be around.

Play even makes it more fun to be YOU.

So you want to play!

But you look out the window, and what do you see? It's raining. Or sleeting. Or maybe you just can't see anything when you look out, because it's pitch dark.

You're stuck indoors. But that doesn't mean you've got to put play on hold. You've got *The Ultimate Indoor Games Book* in your hands! In here are 200 of the best boredom busters ever: games to play with friends or family—or even alone.

Which game?

The games are organized into eight chapters so you can easily find the kind of game you feel like playing. Read Getting Started first. (It begins on the next page.) It tells you how to play any game, and explains what's special about these games. Then pick a game.

Want to play without worrying about equipment? Turn to Just Play. All you need to play dozens of games is yourself, and maybe a friend or two.

Do you want to test yourself or your friends? Races & Relays includes everything from hopping, rolling, and counting races to poetry and swim contests. That's right, swim contests. And you can play one-on-one or in teams.

A pen, some paper, and the Pen & Paper Games chapter is all you need for hours of fun. Stump your friends at word games, race paper airplanes, and more.

Have a full deck of cards? Use them to play both the old-fashioned and the unusual games in the chapter called Card Games. Missing a few cards? Play the card tossing and stacking games.

You don't have to be any sort of athlete to play anything from the collection of Ball Games. You'll find indoor versions of outdoor sports, plus one-of-a-kind games to entertain you and make time fly.

When your body is tired but your mind is still up for a challenge, check out Brain Games. You won't find math problems or spelling bees, just lots of original games to tickle your brain and your funny bone. (Plus a few classic games your parents remember.)

If you've got marbles, coins, or dice handy, turn to the section filled with games played with those objects. (Can you guess what that chapter's called?) Find games that make you laugh, think, or move—then take your pick!

Not sure what you feel like doing? Turn to Oddballs. That chapter has all sorts of games with nothing in common but fun.

Grab a friend, or three, or more. Pick a game (or three, or more.) Then chill out, laugh, and be YOU. In other words, play!

Getting Started

Where to Play

You can play all these games inside your house—even Foot Volleyball, Disc Golf, and lots of fast-moving games. Some games require just the right space for a game to work, and for you to safely play. That's why each game's instructions includes "Where to Play." These range from "anywhere" to "against a wall," and from "in a room" to "in a house."

To play Rock, Paper, Scissors on page 30, you really can be "anywhere"—indoors or out, at your kitchen table, or on a Ferris wheel. For marbles games, play "on a hard floor," because marbles won't roll well on a soft surface, such as a thick carpet.

Anytime a game calls for playing "in a room," you need to read the instructions, and then choose a room. So, for Jump Rope Relay on page 61, don't pick a room with a ceiling fan. If you think you'll make diving catches when you play 500 on page 68, choose a carpeted room. Oh, and you need to choose a space or room where you are allowed to play, move furniture, and remove breakable objects. Always put the room back the way you found it after you finish playing.

If you find a way to make a game more fun or more challenging by changing the play area, go for it. Just make sure all the players know.

Setting Up Boundaries

These aren't the Olympic games, so the boundaries don't have to be perfect. Just make sure all the players know what the boundaries are so everyone can play fair.

If you need Start and Finish lines, or a Base, either use what you have or mark boundaries. That means you can make the floors, walls, and furniture your boundaries. The edge of a table is the Out boundary line when playing Shuffleboard on page 95. And it's obvious, because if your coin slides Out, it falls off the table. If there's a small rug on top of a carpet, say that the rug is Base. You could even move the rug to just the right location as you set up the play area.

To mark boundaries, you can use string, rope, or tape. Pick the right material for the game. For instance, you don't want players in a running relay race to trip over a thick rope. Try string or tape instead. (Always get permission before putting tape on the floor; depending on the surface and the type of tape, you could damage the floor.) Dental floss is the best material to use to mark boundaries for marbles games; the floss is so thin that the marbles easily roll over it without slowing down.

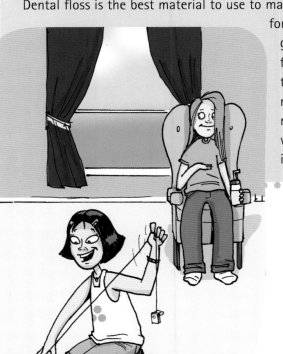

Bringing the Outdoors Indoors

Do you recognize some of the game titles and think of them as outdoor games? Not to worry—the instructions were tweaked to transform fun outdoor games into great indoor games. A good example is Capture the Flag, which you may have played at summer camp. The version of Capture the Flag on page 111 has all the adventure and excitement of the outdoor version, but with less running and no mosquito bites.

Equipment

The instructions for each game include a list of "What You Need." You'll find most of this equipment around the house: playing cards, marbles, a bandana. Because you're inside, surrounded by walls, when you play an active game you're more likely to be hit with equipment or bang into friends and doors and such. So for those games you'll use easy-to-find equipment that works well indoors. That's why Foot Volleyball on page 71 uses a balloon for the ball.

If you don't have the exact piece of equipment recommend, try playing the game using something else that seems suitable.

Rules

Read the rules of a game before you start playing it. Go over these rules with all the players. Agree on how you will play.

One of the best things about playing games is that you can make up your own rules. Just add or change rules before the game starts. Or, if the game is too easy or too hard, call a time-out and figure out what kind of new rules would make the game more fun. Then start the game over.

Choosing Teams

A game lasts longer and is more fun when you have a balance of ages and sizes on each team, instead of having all the older kids or all the strongest players on one team. Keep this in mind as you pick teams using one of these methods:

• Players line up and count off, so that every player says "1" or "2." The 1s are all on a team, and the 2s are on the other.

• Players line up in any order, or line up according to something, such as age, shirt color, or alphabetical order.

• Pick a captain for each team. The captains take turns picking players to be on their teams.

Choosing Referees

Some of the games in this book need a Referee. If you have an extra player waiting a turn to play, have her or him referee. Or ask whether someone wants to take a break from playing and volunteer. You can also try to find an adult to referee. If no one wants to referee, choose someone using any of the Choosing IT methods. Decide how you'll rotate players so that everybody gets to play for a while.

Choosing IT

Being "IT" is fun. And it's easier to catch people when you are IT for an indoor game: the players don't have as much room to run from you! Some of these games require one player to be "IT." There are lots of ways to pick IT. Here are four options:

• Call "Not IT!" The last player to call "Not IT" is IT. You can also do something like touch your nose when saying "Not IT."

• Tear up pieces of paper and mark one with an X. Put the papers into a hat so no one can see which piece he's drawing. The person who gets the X is IT. (This method is perfect for games that require keeping ITs identify secret, such as Winks on page 127.)

• Grab a broom or yardstick. Gather around the broom. Put one hand on the very bottom, nearest the bristles. Quickly, all of the other players place their hands on the broom handle, one hand at a time. The person whose hand is nearest the top of the broomstick is IT.

• Stand in a circle and chant a rhyme. One player points at each player (including herself) on every word. The person who is pointed at on the last word of the rhyme leaves the circle. The rhyme is repeated again and again until only one player remains in the circle. That person is IT.

Being a Good Sport

The point of playing is to have fun. When every player plays fair, plays hard, and has a good time, everyone is happy. Who wins and who loses doesn't matter. If you lose a game, or two, or 10, so what? If you're having fun, you'll play again. For most of these games, determining who won is just a way to decide who goes first next. That doesn't mean you shouldn't be pleased if you win a game through skill, effort, or luck. It's a thrill to win. Just don't rub it in. (Have you noticed that a Bad Sport is rarely invited to play again?)

If one player's skills are much better than the rest of the players, consider making a rule to make it more challenging for that player. So, if you're playing Bocce on page 69 and a much older kid has scored all the points, make a rule that players over a certain age have to play using just one hand—their nondominant hand!

How to End the Game

You can play until a goal is reached, such as tagging everyone or earning 15 points. Either way, figure out before you start playing what the goal is, and how to reach it. (What counts as a point? How many points? What counts as a tag?)

For most of these games, you could play a World Series. Just play an odd-numbered series of games (five, seven, etc.) and see who wins most often. If you don't want to play for a score, play for a specific amount of time, such as "until dinnertime."

Grab your friends, pick a game, play fair, play hard, and have fun!

JUST PLAY

Ready to laugh, hide, wrestle, and more?

Alligator ....

What You Do

1   One player is the Alligator. The player's arms and hands are powerful Alligator jaws full of sharp teeth. These are used to catch the other players.

2   The Alligator kneels in the middle of the hallway. The Alligator can sit on its heels or pop up onto its knees, but can't move its knees from its spot.

3   The other players walk or run past the Alligator, trying to avoid getting caught. (Players can take turns or all try at once.) A player can try to wiggle free, but a capture is complete when the Alligator locks its jaws around a player by clasping its hands.

4   Each captured player sits down behind the Alligator. Play continues until the Alligator captures everyone. The last player caught is the new Alligator.

Other Ways to Play

Blindfolded: Use a bandana to blindfold the Alligator.

Number of Players: 3 or more
What You Need: nothing
Where to Play: in a hallway
The Point: avoid the jaws of the Alligator

Angels

What You Do

1 Two or 3 players are Angels. The Angels move to one side of the room.

2 All the other players are Mortals. The Mortals spread out around the room, find a place to stand, and close both eyes.

3 The Angels count aloud from 1 to 10 to let the Mortals know the game is about to begin. At "10," the Angels quietly move around the room.

4 Each Angel stands as close as possible to a player for 10 seconds. If a Mortal doesn't notice the Angel, the Angel taps the Mortal on the shoulder and the Mortal sits down and is Out. (That Mortal can open both eyes and watch the rest of the players continue the game.)

5 If a Mortal feels an Angel's presence, the Mortal says, "Is there an Angel with me?" If the Mortal is correct, the Angel says so and that Mortal becomes an Angel. If the Mortal is wrong, the Mortal sits down and is Out.

6 Play until everyone is either an Angel or Out.

Number of Players: 6 or more
What You Need: nothing
Where to Play: in a room
The Point: feel the presence of Angels

Number of Players: 2
What You Need: a table and 2 chairs
Where to Play: on a tabletop
The Point: pin your opponent

Arm Wrestling

What You Do

1 Players sit up straight, facing the opponent across the table, or across the corner of the table if the table is large.

2 Players place their right elbows on the table-top, and clasp one another's right hand.

3 When play begins, players use all their arm-strength to force the back of the opponent's right hand onto the tabletop. The right elbows and left hands should not move.

4 A player wins by pinning the opponent's hand to the table.

Belly Laugh

What You Do

1 One player lies down on the floor, with her back on the floor. A second player lies down on the floor, resting her head on the belly of the first player.

2 Players continue lying down in this fashion until everyone is on the floor.

3 The first player laughs, "Ha!" The second player must laugh, "Ha, Ha!" The laugh continues down the line, with each player adding a "Ha."

4 Play until somebody laughs at the wrong time, or the wrong way. Then let another player begin passing the laughter.

Number of Players: 5 or more
What You Need: nothing
Where to Play: in a carpeted room
The Point: keep up with the laughs

Boot Camp

What You Do

1 Players begin by lying face down on the floor. Everyone needs enough room to move around without knocking into another player.

2 Players count aloud together from 1 to 3, and after "3" they move as fast as they can to do 1 push-up, 1 sit-up, and 1 jumping jack.

3 Players then do 2 push-ups, 2 sit-ups, and 2 jumping jacks. After completing each round, the players add 1 repetition to each activity. (1, 2, 3, 4, 5, 6, and so on.) Players shouldn't wait for others to catch up.

4 The player who does the most rounds of push-ups, sit-ups, and jumping jacks wins. That winning number becomes the number to beat in the next game.

Number of Players: 2 or more
What You Need: nothing
Where to Play: in a carpeted room
The Point: best yourself and your friends

Number of Players: 4 or more
What You Need: nothing
Where to Play: anywhere
The Point: get rid of your brother

Brother for Sale

What You Do

1 Pick 1 pair of players. Let them decide which of them is the Brother (or Sister) for Sale and which is the Seller. The Seller and Brother must make the players smile or laugh.

2 The players line up facing the pair. (Give them plenty of room.) The Seller then picks 1 player at a time to "sell" the Brother.

3 The Seller says, "Will you buy my Brother? He's a good Brother, he can..." The Seller fills in the blank with an action that the Brother then has to do. Break-dancing, singing, and juggling shoes are all things a good Brother might do.

4 If the player being asked smiles or laughs during the demonstration, he becomes the new Brother for Sale! Otherwise, he says, "No, thank you." Then the Seller tries to sell the Brother to another player.

Bubble Gum

What You Do

1. Players gather in a circle, sitting or standing. One player is the Rhymer. Everyone makes 2 fists and extends them into the center of the circle.

2. The Rhymer uses 1 fist to tap each player's fists, one at a time, while saying this rhyme, "Bubble gum, bubble bum, in a dish. How many pieces do you wish?" (The Rhymer's fists are also tapped.)

3. Whoever's fist is tapped on "wish" says a number between 1 and 11. The Rhymer then counts out that many taps on the fists. The last fist tapped is out of the game. (The player moves it behind the back.) The Rhymer says the rhyme while tapping, and play continues.

4. The last player in the game wins.

Bumper Cars

What You Do

1. Players squat and tuck their arms behind their thighs so that each hand crosses under and reaches the opposite side. (Players can tuck their arms behind their knees, if that's more comfortable.)

2. When everyone's ready, play begins and each player waddles around, trying to bump the other over. No elbowing or headbutting allowed. Players have to hold the squat position.

3. The first player to knock over all the others wins.

Can't Move Me...

What You Do

1. Players stand and face one another. Each player extends the right foot so that it touches the outside edge of the other player's right foot.

2. Players clasp each other's right hand, as if shaking hands, and put their left arms behind their backs. Players bend both legs slightly, for balance, and choose a stance.

3. When play begins, players push, pull, and shake the opponent's right hand in an attempt to make the opponent move. The first player to make the other take a step or move the left arm wins.

Other Ways to Play

Switch: Have each player extend the left foot, clasp the opponent's left hand, and put the right hand behind the back.

Number of Players: 2
What You Need: nothing
Where to Play: in a carpeted room
The Point: topple your opponent

Number of Players: 8 or more
What You Need: nothing
Where to Play: in a room
The Point: sit down in a circle

Chair

What You Do

1. Players stand in a circle, shoulder to shoulder and facing the center of the circle.

2. Players all turn to the right and count aloud from 1 to 3. After "3," players all sit down on the knees of the person behind. Everyone sits at the same time, but slowly.

3. Try as many times as it takes to get it right!

Other Ways to Play

Forward: After mastering how to sit as a circle, players stay in a seated position and take a step forward.
Backward: After mastering how to sit and take a step forward as a group, the players all take a step backwards.

Flamingos

What You Do

1 Players stand facing one another. Each player extends the right arm and hand, and grasps the opponent's extended right hand.

2 It will look as if the players are shaking hands. Then each player bends the left leg, lifts the ankle toward the back, and grasps the left ankle with the left hand. (Bending the right leg helps with balance.) The stance of both players should now resemble flamingos.

3 To play, players tug and twist their arms to unbalance the opponent. The player who makes the other let go of an ankle or break the handhold wins.

Number of Players: 2
What You Need: nothing
Where to Play: in a carpeted room
The Point: unbalance the other bird

Other Ways to Play

Opposite: Players grasp one another's left hand and hold the right ankle with the right hand.

Follow the Leader

What You Do

1 Pick a player to be the Leader. All of the other players line up behind the Leader.

2 The Leader starts walking, skipping, or whatever. All of the other players must do the same thing. For instance, if the Leader scrunches down and unties and reties a shoelace, all of the other players must do the same, the exact same way.

3 After a set time, the Leader goes to the back of the line. The player in front is the new Leader.

Number of Players: 2 or more
What You Need: nothing
Where to Play: in a room·
The Point: imitate what you see

Friend or Foe?

What You Do

1 One player is IT. The other players stand in a circle and join hands. These joined players are Friends.

2 To begin the game, IT runs around the circle and picks a pair of hands to tap. These two players are now Foes.

3 Each Foe runs in the opposite direction of the opponent, all the way around the circle, racing to rejoin the circle first. Meanwhile, IT becomes a Friend and joins the circle.

4 The last foe to reach the open spot is the new IT.

Number of Players: 6 or more
What You Need: nothing
Where to Play: in a room
The Point: rejoin your Friends

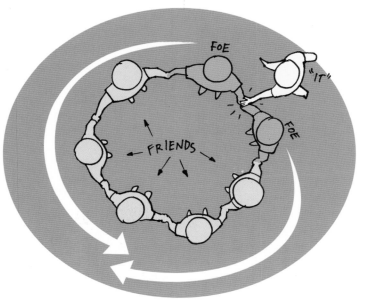

Frighteningly Freaky Fingers

Number of Players: 4 or more
What You Need: bandana
Where to Play: in a room
The Point: keep quiet

What You Do

1 One player is IT. IT leaves the room and begins counting to 22. All the other players hide in the room. (To make the game spooky, turn out the lights.)

2 IT yells, "22, 22, Freaky Fingers are coming to find you." IT then closes both eyes, puts on the bandana as a blindfold, and reenters the room to search for players. IT should reach out and poke around dramatically with ITs Freaky Fingers. Players can't move!

3 Players should be quiet—IT can't see, but IT can hear. The last player found and touched by IT becomes the new IT.

Ghost

Number of Players: 3 or more
What You Need: nothing
Where to Play: in a house
The Point: outrun the Ghost

What You Do

1 The players pick someone to be the Ghost and agree on a Base. All the players stand on or touch Base, close their eyes, and count down aloud each hour from 1 p.m. to midnight. Meanwhile, the Ghost hides.

2 The players yell, "Midnight," and search for the Ghost. The first to see the Ghost yells, "Ghost," and the players race back to Base before being tagged by the Ghost.

3 The first player tagged becomes the Ghost.

Other Ways to Play

Recruiting: Each caught player becomes a Ghost, and play continues until everyone is a Ghost.

Hazing

Number of Players: 6 or more
What You Need: nothing
Where to Play: in a room
The Point: play it cool

What You Do

1 One player is the Pledge and stands in the center of the room. All the other players are part of the Clique. The Clique divides in half, standing in lines on either side of the Pledge.

2 The Pledge wants to join the Clique, but can only do so by slowly walking past its members without smiling or laughing. The Clique members can't touch the Pledge, but can make faces and say things to make the Pledge smile or laugh.

3 A Pledge gets 3 chances to win. Then someone else gets to be the new Pledge.

Hide and Seek

Number of Players: 2 or more
What You Need: good places to hide
Where to Play: anywhere
The Point: hide well

What You Do

1 Players choose a Base and a player to be IT. IT stands at Base, covers ITs eyes, and counts to 30. All of the other players move away and hide.

2 IT calls out, "Ready or not, here I come!" and looks for the others. IT calls out the name of any player it spots, then tries to tag her before she touches Base.

3 The last player caught wins.

Hot Lava

What You Do

1. The floor in every room of the house is Hot Lava. One player is the Leader. The other players follow the Leader through the house, but no one can touch the Hot Lava.

2. This means you're climbing on furniture, stepping on anything on the floor that is not the floor. (So players should agree whether or not rugs are part of the Hot Lava.)

3. If the Leader gets stuck and can't find a route—or steps in Hot Lava, a player with an idea for continuing becomes the new Leader.

Number of Players: 2 or more
What You Need: nothing
Where to Play: in a house
The Point: step over the molten rock

I Don't Believe in Ghosts

What You Do

1 Players turn out all the lights, pull the curtains, and agree on a route through as many rooms as possible in the darkened house. The route should be a continuous loop. (No dead-ends.)

2 One player is the Ghost and hides somewhere along the route. The rest of the players put hands on either sides of their faces to shield their eyes (like blinders on a horse). No peeking. The players then walk the route through the house, saying aloud, "I don't believe in ghosts."

3 Meanwhile, the Ghost sneaks up behind the players and picks one to surprise and grab. That player becomes the new Ghost, and the game continues. Soon, no one knows who the Ghost is, except the Ghost!

Number of Players: 5 or more
What You Need: nothing
Where to Play: in a dark house
The Point: frighten or be frightened

In or Out?

What You Do

1 Players agree on a line in the room, or mark one with a string. One player is the Leader. The other players all line up on the same side of the agreed-upon line.

2 The Leader tells the players which side of the line is "In" and which is "Out." To begin the game, the Leader counts from 1 to 3 out loud, then begins calling out "In" or "Out." The players must jump where they are told. (Sometimes this means a player just jumps up, instead of jumping over the line.) Anyone who messes up is out of the game.

3 The last player in the game becomes the new Leader.

Number of Players: 4 or more
What You Need: string (optional)
Where to Play: anywhere
The Point: listen closely

Knots

What You Do

1 All of the players stand in a circle, facing each other. Everybody puts his or her hands into the center.

2 Each player grabs one hand each from two other players, following these rules: a player can't hold both hands of the same player, and a player can't hold hands with either player to the immediate right or left in the circle.

Number of Players: 5 or more
What You Need: nothing
Where to Play: anywhere
The Point: untangle yourselves

3 Once all the players are holding hands, start to untangle the knot. Players can step over and under other players' arms. Players can't let go of each other's hands.

4 The game is over when everyone is standing in a circle again.

Lay a Hand On

Number of Players: 4 or more
What You Need: nothing
Where to Play: in a room
The Point: reach for the right thing

What You Do

1. One player is the Caller. The Caller stands aside while the other players sit in a circle. Players can't leave the circle.

2. When everyone is in place, the Caller starts the game by telling the players the first "thing" they must touch. Everything called must be found within reach of the circle. So, if a player is wearing red shoes, the Caller might say, "Lay a hand on red." Everyone will have to touch the shoes—unless they find something else red (such as someone's hair).

3. The Caller should keep changing what the players are touching. Be creative. "Lay a hand on soft." (A belly?) "Lay a hand on Tyler." (Watch out, Tyler!)

4. The Caller keeps watch for players who don't move fast enough. (The Caller decides what is "fast enough.") Those players are out of the game.

5. The last player in the game becomes the new Caller.

Lazybones

Number of Players: 3 or more
What You Need: nothing
Where to Play: in a room
The Point: rouse the Lazybones

What You Do

1. One player is the Motivational Speaker. (That's a person who encourages others to do something besides being a Lazybones.) All the other players are Lazybones.

2. The Lazybones lie down, stretch out, or curl up in the room. They can keep their eyes open, but they cannot move.

3. To win, the Motivational Speaker needs to rouse all the Lazybones, making the Lazybones move just by talking to them. Smiling is moving, and so is changing position.

4. The last Lazybones to move is the next Motivational Speaker.

Leg Wrestling

What You Do

1 Players lie on the floor, their heads facing in opposite directions. Legs and arms are out-stretched down alongside their bodies, nearly touching the opponent. Players' backs must remain flat against the floor throughout the game.

2 Players link arms at the elbow, using the nearest arm. The other arm remains on the floor.

3 Players extend the leg nearest the opponent straight up toward the ceiling, and then link this leg behind the knee of the opponent's extended leg.

4 On the count of 3, the game begins and players wrestle, using only their linked legs and arms.

5 A player wins by forcing the opponent's back off the floor.

Number of Players: 2 of similar size
What You Need: nothing
Where to Play: on a carpeted floor
The Point: outmuscle the competition

Part to Part

What You Do

1. One player is the Caller. The other players pair up. (Any extra player can join in during step 3.)

2. The Caller calls out 2 arm or leg parts at a time and each pair must put those parts together. For instance, "ankle to wrist," and then "elbow to knee," then "fingers to foot."

3. At any time, the Caller can say, "people to people." That means all players have to find a new partner as quickly as possible, including the Caller. Whichever player does not get a partner becomes the new Caller.

Number of Players: 5 or more
What You Need: nothing
Where to Play: in a room
The Point: make silly connections

Pinkie Pairs

What You Do

1. Players pair up, stand back to back with their hands to their sides, and then link their pinkies.

2. Each pair must lower to the floor, pressing against the back of the partner. Pairs go all the way to the floor, until both players are sitting, and then get back up. Backsides must touch the whole time. Pinkies can't come unlinked.

3. The pairs of players who succeed are the winners.

Number of Players: 2 or more
What You Need: nothing
Where to Play: in a room
The Point: slide down, then up

Rock, Paper, Scissors

What You Do

1 Players can "throw" 1 of 3 gestures in this game. The possible throws are Rock, formed by making a fist; Paper, formed by flattening the hand, palm down; or Scissors, formed by opening the first and index fingers to resemble a pair of scissors.

2 Rock always breaks Scissors to win, Paper always covers Rock to win, and Scissors always cuts Paper to win. Players can also tie by throwing the same gesture.

3 Players face one another and count out loud together from 1 to 3, each player hitting 1 fist into the palm of the other hand on each count.

4 After the third hit, each player "throws" a gesture, using 1 hand. The winner does the count for the next game. If the players tie, those players throw again.

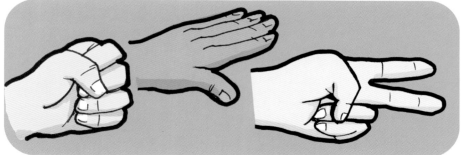

Sardines

What You Do

1 Players agree on a Base and choose the 1 player who will go hide. All the other players stand at Base, cover their eyes, and count to 30.

2 When the other players are done counting, everyone separates and looks for the hiding spot. Each player who finds the hiding spot squeezes in to hide, too.

3 The last one to find the hiding spot is chased back to Base by the rest of the players. If that player is caught, she becomes the next player to hide. Otherwise, the second-to-last player who found the hiding spot hides next.

Shipshape

What You Do

1. The room is a Ship. One player is the Captain. The other players are the Pirates.

2. The game begins when the Captain says, "All Pirates on deck." That means all players need to stand up for duty. The Captain will give the following orders:

   Hit the deck: Lay down on the floor
   Stern: Run to the back
   Row your boat: The Captain points to 3 players and they sing, "Row, Row, Row Your Boat"
   Clear the deck: Pirates can't touch the floor with their feet
   Starboard: Run to the right side
   Port: Run to the left side
   Bow: Run to the front
   Attention: Salute and say, "Aye, aye, Captain"

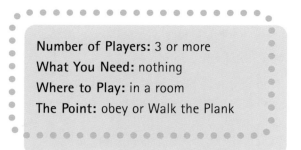

Number of Players: 3 or more
What You Need: nothing
Where to Play: in a room
The Point: obey or Walk the Plank

3. If the Captain sees a Pirate not following orders, the Captain orders the Pirate to Walk the Plank, and he's Out. The last Pirate becomes the new Captain.

Snakebite

What You Do

1. Players form a line and hold the waist of the player in front, just like in a conga dance line.

2. The player at the front of the line is the Snake's Head. The player at the end of the line is the Snake's Tail. The Head tries to bite (grab the waist of) the Tail, and the Tail and the rest of the snake try to stay out of reach.

3. Each player takes a turn being the Snake's Head and Tail.

Number of Players: 5 or more
What You Need: nothing
Where to Play: in a large room
The Point: avoid a Snakebite

Snarky

Number of Players: 4 or more
What You Need: nothing
Where to Play: anywhere
The Point: make everyone laugh

What You Do

1. Players stand or sit in a circle, and one starts the game by making a funny face. The goal is to make the other players laugh. The player "passes" this face clockwise to the next player. Players pass it on.

2. Anyone who laughs is Out of the game and takes a step back. The rest of the players move in to make a smaller circle.

3. After the face moves around the circle back to where it began, the player to the left creates a new face and passes it.

4. Play continues until there's only 1 player still in the game. (If there's a stalemate, 2 people win.)

Snake in the Grass

Number of Players: 6 or more
What You Need: nothing
Where to Play: in a carpeted room
The Point: outrun a Snake

What You Do

1. One player is the Snake and lies in the middle of the room, stomach on the floor. The floor is the Grass.

2. The other players walk into the Grass as if they can't see the Snake. The players should walk around and over the Snake, who is invisible in the Grass.

3. At any time, the Snake can yell, "Snake in the Grass." The players should run away as quickly as possible. Meanwhile, the Snake has 3 seconds to reach around and grab players while keeping its belly on the floor.

4. Anyone who touches the Snake or is touched by the Snake becomes another Snake. Play until everyone is a Snake. The last player tagged is the first Snake in the next game.

Sock Wrestling

What You Do

1. Two at a time, players pair up and take off their shoes. Pairs can sit or stand, but it's easiest to start the game sitting on your heels.

2. Players count aloud together from 1 to 3. On "3" they begin trying to take off the opponent's socks.

3. The first player to get both socks off the opponent's feet wins.

Number of Players: 2 or more
What You Need: socks on your feet
Where to Play: in a carpeted room
The Point: remove your opponent's socks

Statues

What You Do

1 Pick the first player to be the Sculptor. The Sculptor twirls each player around, one at a time. When the Sculptor stops twirling a player, the player freezes into a Statue.

2 Players hold their positions until all the players have been turned into Statues.

3 The Sculptor walks from Statue to Statue, trying to make each one laugh or move. The last player to laugh or move is the next Sculptor.

Other Ways to Play

What kind: The Sculptor can tell the players what sorts of sculptures they should be, such as types of animals.

Number of Players: 4 or more
What You Need: nothing
Where to Play: anywhere
The Point: hold your pose

Number of Players: 3 or more
What You Need: string (optional)
Where to Play: in a wide hallway or room
The Point: reach IT

Stop and Go

What You Do

1 Pick the first player to be IT and mark the Start Line. IT stands far away from all the other players, who are lined up behind the Start Line.

2 IT calls out, "green light," and turns ITs back to the players. The players begin moving toward IT. When IT calls out "red light," IT spins and faces the players—who freeze. Anyone IT catches moving goes back to Start. Then IT calls out, "green light," again, and so on.

3 The first player to touch IT wins and becomes the new IT.

Super Duck

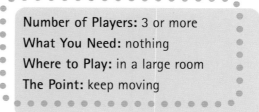

Number of Players: 4 or more
What You Need: nothing
Where to Play: in a house
The Point: be a superhero, or foil one!

What You Do

1 Players agree on a playing area, such as 3 connected rooms in the house. Players pick someone to be IT, and IT picks a space to be the Prison, such as on an area rug in the kitchen.

2 All the players stand in the Prison, or with at least 1 foot in. While IT closes both eyes and counts aloud to 10, the other players run from the Prison and hide. After reaching "10," IT hunts for the players.

3 When IT sees or touches a player, that player must go to the Prison. At any time a Prisoner can call out, "This is a job for Super Duck." Any other player can reply with a loud, "quack quack." This frees the Prisoner. But look out, because now IT has a clue to Super Duck's whereabouts!

4 IT wins by capturing all the players.

Tag

Number of Players: 3 or more
What You Need: nothing
Where to Play: in a large room
The Point: keep moving

What You Do

1 Pick a person to be IT. IT must crawl on all fours, and begins play in the middle of the room.

2 The other players line up against one end of the room. That wall is Start. The opposite wall is Base. Players must alternate touching Base and Start—by getting past IT. (A player who fails to alternate touching Base and Start is automatically IT!)

3 IT tags players, and wherever IT touches a player, the player has to stick her hand there. For instance, IT could tag her ankle. She can move, but she has to keep the hand on her ankle until another player touches the same spot and "frees" the "stuck" hand.

4 IT can tag any player who has a "free" hand—unless she's touching Start or Base. Being tagged 3 times makes a player the next IT!

Thumbs Up

What You Do

1 The players close their eyes and count out loud together from 1 to 3. On "3," the players stick both fists out and do 1 of the following things: stick up 1 thumb, 2 thumbs, or no thumbs.

2 With eyes still closed, each player quickly calls out a number that is a guess of how many thumbs will be up.

3 The players all open their eyes and count the thumbs. Whomever guessed correctly wins.

Number of Players: 4 or more
What You Need: nothing
Where to Play: anywhere
The Point: guess well

Number of Players: 2
What You Need: nothing
Where to Play: on a table
The Point: pin the opponent's thumb

Thumb Wrestling

What You Do

1 Each player makes a fist with the right hand and rests the right forearm on the table. The hand is pinky-side down.

2 Players open those fists just enough to grip the opponent's fingers. Each player rests a thumb near the knuckle of his index finger.

3 The players count down aloud together from 3. On "3," the Wrestling begins. The right hands must remain clasped, and the right forearms must remain on the table.

4 The first player to pin the other's thumb and hold it for a count of 3 wins.

Other Ways to Play

Declaration: Recite, "1, 2, 3, 4, I declare a thumb war!" while giving alternating thumb taps to each right index-finger knuckle. Then start Wrestling.

Ultimate Kick-Off

Number of Players: 2 or more
What You Need: nothing
Where to Play: in a room
The Point: "kick" a winning move

What You Do

1 Two players compete at a time. The players stand and face one another, leaving a few feet of space between them. One player is called "Odd" and the other is called "Even."

2 The players count aloud together from 1 to 3 and jump up on each count. After saying, "3," each player "kicks" one of 2 moves: stick out the right foot or stick out the left foot.

3 If the players' feet are lined up with each other, they're "even" and Even wins the round. (This happens when 1 player kicks out a right foot and the other player kicks out a left foot.) If the players' feet are at a diagonal, they're "odd" and Odd wins the round. (This happens when both players kick out their right feet, or both kick out their left feet.)

4 The winner does the count for the next game.

Wily Knights

Number of Players: 2 or more
What You Need: nothing
Where to Play: in a room
The Point: score points with finger swords

What You Do

1 Players pair up and stand facing one another. (An extra player can play against the winner of the first game.)

2 Players put one hand behind their backs, laying the back of the hand flat against the back, with the palm open. This is the Knight's Shield. The index finger of the other hand is the Knight's Sword.

3 To play, each Knight tries to strike the opponent's Shield with her Sword. Touching any part of the opponent's palm counts as a strike and earns 1 point.

4 The first Knight to earn 7 points wins.

BRAIN GAMES

Think fast, think hard, think fun!

3-Letter Words

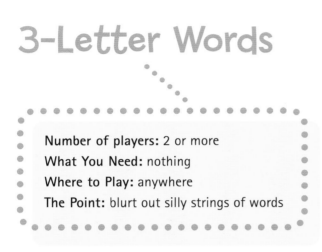

> **Number of players:** 2 or more
> **What You Need:** nothing
> **Where to Play:** anywhere
> **The Point:** blurt out silly strings of words

What You Do

1 One player says a 3-letter word, and then creates a sentence or string of words using the letters of the word. For instance, "Dog: Did Opal go?"

2 Play passes to the left, with each player using that same word and making up a new sentence or string of words. Players who mess up are Out.

3 The last person to take a turn without messing up wins and gets to pick the next 3-letter word to play with.

Other Ways to Play

Lightning round: Choose a timekeeper to limit each player to only 10 seconds, or less, to respond.
Add letters: Use 4- or 5-letter words.
Go backward: Create a backward sentence or phrase. For instance, "Dog: Go out, Doug."

A What?

What You Do

1. The players sit in a circle. One player begins the game by passing an object to the left, announcing that it's something completely different. For instance, pass a football while saying, "This is a hot extra-cheese pizza."

2. The second player must ask, "A what?" The first player repeats, "A hot extra-cheese pizza." The second player then takes the object and passes it to the next player, using the same dialogue. ("This is a hot extra-cheese pizza." "A what?" "A hot extra-cheese pizza.")

3. The first object keeps going around the circle, but now the first player adds a second object to the game, passing it in either direction. Again, the object is called something it's not. (Make sure you call it something silly and complicated.) Now 2 objects are being passed.

4. Keep adding objects and passing them until everyone is laughing.

Animal, Vegetable, Mineral

What You Do

1 One player is the Answerer, and the others are all Guessers. The Answerer picks the subject of the game, which must fall under 1 of these categories: Animal, Vegetable, or Mineral.

Animal: an actual animal (including a specific person) or any thing made from an animal (Swiss cheese, shoes)

Vegetable: an actual vegetable, or things made from vegetables (paper, clothes, French fries)

Mineral: everything else (The Statue of Liberty, roads, air)

Number of Players: 3 or more
What You Need: nothing
Where to Play: anywhere
The Point: figure out the answer

2 The Guessers try to figure out the subject by taking turns asking a total of 20 questions that receive only a "yes" or "no" response from the Answerer.

3 After all 20 questions are asked, each Guesser takes a turn guessing what the subject is. The winner is the first Guesser to get it right.

Antidisestablishmentarianism

What You Do

1 One player is IT. Players take turns asking IT questions. ITs only answer to every question is, "Antidisestablishmentarianism."

2 That's "an-ti-dis-es-tab-lish-men-tar-ian-ism." (Why did the chicken cross the road? "Antidisestablishmentarianism.")

3 The first player to make IT mess up saying the word or laugh becomes the new IT.

Number of Players: 3 or more
What You Need: nothing
Where to Play: anywhere
The Point: make IT laugh or mess up

Other Ways to Play

Soysage: Use "soysage" or another funny word as the answer to all the questions.

Bean Soup

What You Do

1. One player is IT and stands in the center of the room. The other players stand in a line near IT.

2. IT assigns a unique vegetable name to each player, such as green beans, okra, and so on. Players must remember their names.

3. To begin the game, IT announces, "Green Beans and Okra, switch places."

4. While the players called on move as quickly as possible to switch places, IT tries to take 1 of their spots.

5. Whoever doesn't get a spot becomes IT.

Number of Players: 2 or more
What You Need: nothing
Where to Play: in a room
The Point: pass the sound

Number of Players: 7 or more
What You Need: nothing
Where to Play: in a room
The Point: mix the soup without getting left out

Beep-Beep, Buzz-Buzz

What You Do

1. The players sit in a circle. There are 2 sounds and 2 ways to pass them. Beep-beep: put a hand on the head with a finger pointing straight ahead. Buzz-buzz: put a hand under the chin and point a finger right or left.

2. One player starts the game by passing a sound. The player pointed at must catch it by doing the same action, and then quickly pass a sound with the other hand. Players use only 1 hand at a time.

3. If a player messes up, she starts again. Everyone wins when the whole group completes a pass.

Campfire

What You Do

1. Players sit in a circle. One player is the Leader. The other players are the Campers. The Leader begins a story of a hike and the Campers use their hands to make the sound of what the Leader describes. These are the sounds:

   Walking: Campers slap their legs in a slow, steady rhythm no faster than what it takes to say "one-one-thousand."

   Crossing a bridge: Campers slap their hands on the floor instead of their legs.

   Climbing a mountain: Campers slap their hands together over their heads.

   Swimming across a river: Campers make swimming motions with their hands.

Number of Players: 3 or more
What You Need: nothing
Where to Play: anywhere
The Point: race to camp with your hands

2. At any time, the Leader can say the Campers ran into a bear. The Campers must race back to camp by traveling the same ways and making the right sounds and movements in the correct reverse order.

3. The first Camper to get back to camp is the new Leader.

Number of Players: 4 or more
What You Need: a bandana
Where to Play: in a room
The Point: disguise your voice

Captain, O Captain

What You Do

1. One player is the Captain. The other players are Mateys. (As in, "Aye, Mateys!")

2. The Captain sits in the center of the room and is blindfolded by the Mateys. One at a time, a Matey disguises his voice and says, "Captain, O Captain." The Captain must turn toward the voice and say, "Good morning, _____," filling in the blank with the name of the Matey.

3. If the Captain guesses wrong, the speaker becomes the Captain. Play until everyone has a turn as the Captain.

Count Down

What You Do

1 Players count backward and out loud from 100, by 1s. (100, 99, 98, 97, etc.) All players count at the same time. That's what makes the game hard.

2 Anyone who messes up must start over at 100 again. It doesn't matter how many times players must start over.

3 A player wins by counting down to 0 without a mistake.

Other Ways to Play

Take turns: Players can take turns if they have trouble counting all at the same time. Just remember the last number each player counted correctly. Let the player who gets closest to 0 be the winner.
By 2s: Count backward by 2s. (100, 98, 96, 94, etc.)
By 5s: Count backward by 5s. (100, 95, 90, 85, etc.)

Number of Players: 2 or more
What You Need: nothing
Where to Play: anywhere
The Point: think in reverse

Fly's Eye

What You Do

1. One player is the Fly. The other players are Swatters. Everyone sits at one end of the room, where they can easily see the whole room.

2. The Fly secretly picks a spot in the room. (Don't stare or you'll reveal the spot.) The Swatters take turns asking questions about what the Fly can see from there.

3. After each Swatter has asked 1 question, the Swatters take turns making a guess where the Fly is. The first player to guess correctly becomes the new Fly.

Number of Players: 3 or more
What You Need: nothing
Where to Play: in a room
The Point: find the Fly

Hurrah!

What You Do

1. Pick a player to be IT. IT goes away from all the other players while they huddle and agree on a pose, such as sitting with legs crossed, lying down with one leg in the air, etc.

2. When the other players are ready, IT comes back and slowly begins moving ITs arms, legs, and body into different positions. If IT's getting close to the agreed-on position, all the other players clap and cheer. If IT's not, the players boo.

3. When IT finally gets the pose right, the players cheer wildly and shout "Hurrah!"

Number of Players: 3 or more
What You Need: nothing
Where to Play: anywhere
The Point: decipher the cheers and boos

I'm Going on Vacation

What You Do

1 At least 2 players need to know the trick to this game before play begins. One of these players is the Leader. The others are Tricksters. All the players sit in circle.

2 The Leader begins by saying, "I'm going on a vacation and I'm going to bring ..." The Leader finishes the sentence with any vacation item, such as "sunblock."

3 A Trickster then takes a turn, saying, "I'm going on vacation and I'm going to bring..." The Trickster must name something that begins with the last letter of the last word the Leader said. In this case, that letter is "k," so, the Trickster could say, "a karaoke machine."

Number of Players: 5 or more
What You Need: 2 players who know the trick
Where to Play: anywhere
The Point: figure out the trick

4 Each player takes a turn and tries to figure out the trick to giving a correct answer. If any player doesn't use the correct letter, the Leader and Tricksters say, "No, you can't bring that on vacation."

5 Play until everyone figures out the trick.

Isbot's Gossip Game

Number of Players: 6 or more
What You Need: nothing
Where to Play: anywhere
The Point: pass the message

What You Do

1 Players sit in a circle. One player is the Caller. The rest are all Gossips.

2 The Caller starts the game by whispering a message into the ear of the Gossip seated to the left. (Tongue twisters are fun messages; so are fake stories about the Gossips.)

3 Each Gossip passes the message around the circle, saying it just once to the next Gossip.

4 When the message reaches the Gossip to the right of the Caller, that Gossip says the message out loud.

I Spy

....

. . . .
Number of Players: 2 or more
What You Need: nothing
Where to Play: anywhere
The Point: follow the clues
. . . .

What You Do

1 One player is the Spy. The Spy looks around and chooses an object, but doesn't tell anyone or draw anyone's attention to it.

2 The Spy gives a hint about the object. For instance, if the Spy has chosen a green newt, the Spy could say, "I spy something green."

3 The other players take 1 turn each guessing what object the Spy is talking about. If no one guesses correctly, the Spy gives another simple clue, such as using a word that describes the object. For instance, "I spy something that's not human."

4 Each time the Spy gives a hint, each player gets 1 chance to guess what the object is. The first player to guess correctly wins.

. . . .
Number of Players: 3 or more
What You Need: nothing
Where to Play: anywhere
The Point: reveal the lies
. . . .

Lies & Truths

What You Do

1 Players take turns telling 2 Truths and 1 Lie. The person taking a turn is the Confessor. The Confessor should decide what to say and then tell the Truths and Lie in any order.

2 The game is really fun when you pick Truths that your friends don't know, and a Lie that sounds ordinary. For instance, "I swam naked in the city pool," "I like butter on mashed potatoes," and "I am named after my aunt." (The answers are True (but I was only 2 years old!), False (butter is gross!), True (she was my great-aunt, but that's still an aunt).

3 The other players have to agree on 1 guess about which of the 3 is the Lie. If the players are correct, 1 of them takes a turn as Confessor. If they are wrong, the Confessor gets another turn.

No Way

What You Do

1. Pick a player to be the Talker and stand at one end of the room. Everyone else is a Walker and lines up side by side at the opposite end of the room.

2. Each Walker wants to get to the Talker first, and the Talker wants to keep all the Walkers away. When play begins, each Walker takes a turn asking, "Talker, may I take a step?"

3. The Talker can say "Yes" or "No," but can't say "No" the same way twice. If the talker can't find a new way to say "No" within 5 seconds, the Talker has to say, "Yes." Then that Walker may take 1 step of any size.

4. A Talker wins by keeping the Walkers away. A Walker wins by making the Talker say "No" the same way twice.

Other Ways to Play

Nein: Say no in other languages. Nein (German), Geen (Dutch), Non (French), Ingen (Norwegian).

> Number of Players: 3 or more
> What You Need: nothing
> Where to Play: in a room or wide hallway
> The Point: stretch your vocabulary

Poodle

What You Do

1. One player is the Poodler. The Poodler chooses an action, such as "bicycling" or "thinking," but keeps it a secret.

2. When the Poodler is ready, the other players take turns asking the Poodler "yes" and "no" questions to figure out the action. Players might ask, "Can anyone Poodle?" "Does Poodling hurt?" Or "Do you Poodle in public?"

> Number of Players: 3 or more
> What You Need: nothing
> Where to Play: anywhere
> The Point: figure out what a Poodle is

3. Each player can make a guess after asking a question. The first player to figure out what a Poodle is wins and is the new Poodler.

Rainstorm

Number of Players: 4 or more
What You Need: nothing
Where to Play: in a room
The Point: re-create a storm inside

What You Do

1 Players stand in a circle. One player is the Rain-maker. The Rainmaker begins the game by making a sound that you hear during a rainstorm: falling rain, gusts of wind, thunder, etc. Make the sounds in your throat, or with your fingers or hands, or by stomping your feet, etc.

2 The sound passes around the circle to the left, and each player makes the sound the same way until everyone in the circle is making the same sound. Then the Rainmaker creates a new sound, and it moves around the circle.

3 After at least one round of play, any player may yell "Kaboom" to make lightning strike. When someone yells, "Kaboom," everyone falls down. The fastest player to the floor is the new Rainmaker.

So You Think You Know Your ABCs?

What You Do

1 Players begin by saying, "So you think you know your ABCs?" and then recite the alphabet—backward. All players speak at the same time.

2 Anyone who messes up must start again, repeating, "So you think you know your ABCs?"

3 A player wins by getting to the letter A without a mistake.

Other Ways to Play

Take turns: Players can take turns if they have trouble reciting their ABCs all at the same time. Just remember the last letter each player recited correctly. Let the player who gets closest to the letter A be the winner.

Number of Players: 2 or more
What You Need: nothing
Where to Play: anywhere
The Point: reverse the alphabet

Story

What You Do

1 Players stand or sit in a circle. One player is the Storyteller. All the other players are Characters.

2 The game begins when the Storyteller starts telling a story, making it up on the spot. For every Character in the story, the Storyteller points to a player. That player becomes that Character.

3 Every time a Character is mentioned, the player representing that Character has to act out what is happening while walking once around the circle. Walking around the circle gives the Character more room to pantomime the action. The Storyteller can also say "all," and all the Characters have to act out and walk around the circle.

4 When the story is over, pick a new Storyteller.

Number of Players: 5 or more
What You Need: nothing
Where to Play: in a room
The Point: listen for your role and play your part

Undercover

What You Do

1 Tear off 1 scrap of paper per player. Mark an X on 1 scrap. Put the scraps in a hat and have each player draw a scrap. The player who draws the X is the Undercover Agent, but shouldn't tell anyone.

2 Players spread out around the room, sitting or kneeling. No player can leave the room during play.

3 When the game begins, everyone closes their eyes and begins crawling around the room.

4 When a player finds another player, the player whispers to the other "Undercover Agent?" All players who are not the Agent whisper back, "Undercover Agent," and keep moving. (An Undercover Agent would never admit to being an Agent!)

5 If the real Agent is asked, "Undercover Agent"? the Agent is silent and lays a hand on the other player. This indicates that they are now an undercover team. The team moves around the room and adds more Agents.

6 The game ends when everyone has become an Undercover Agent.

Wolfgang Amadeus Mozart

What You Do

1 Players sit in a circle for this word passing game. One player starts the game by looking at another player and saying, "Wolfgang."

2 It's now that player's turn either to look at a different player and say, "Wolfgang," or to send the turn back to the first player by looking away and saying, "Amadeus." Players should say something as quickly as possible.

3 If a turn is sent back to a player, the player who received it can then say, "Wolfgang" (while looking at a different player), or say "Mozart," looking anywhere and sending the turn back to the player who said "Amadeus."

4 Let everyone have a turn and play until everyone is hopelessly confused.

Zombie

What You Do

1 One player is a Zombie. Every other player is a Corpse. The Zombie is hunting for Corpses that aren't really dead.

2 Before the game begins, the Corpses spread out around the room and lie down. Corpses avoid capture by not moving.

3 The Zombie can't touch the Corpses, but the Zombie can talk to Corpses to make them move. Laughing, smiling, opening your eyes, and cringing are all moves.

4 If the Zombie sees a Corpse move, the Zombie captures the Corpse and it becomes a Zombie. The new Zombie helps the first Zombie search for more moving Corpses.

Number of Players: 3 or more
What You Need: nothing
Where to Play: in a room
The Point: keep still or be turned into a Zombie

BRAINTH... I NEED BRAINTHS...

HMFFF... ~SNICKER~

RACES & RELAYS

Compete with your brain, hands, or feet.

Balloon Smack

What You Do

1 Players line up single-file against the wall on one side of the room. Players will walk to the opposite wall, so they need a clear path.

2 When the race begins, each player has a balloon and the players begin walking at the same time. For each step taken, a player must smack the balloon up into the air with one or both hands. It's a challenge to match the size of your steps and the power of your hits.

3 If a balloon touches the ground, the player returns to Start. The first player to reach the opposite wall wins.

Other Ways to Play

Alternate hands: Alternate using right and left hands.

Bounce-In

What You Do

1 The players divide into 2 teams of Bouncers. If there's an extra player, let that person be the Referee who also chases down loose balls.

2 Each team gets 1 ball and 1 trash can. Place the trash cans 5 or more feet away and have players stand behind a Bounce Line. Use a string to mark the line, if necessary.

3 When everyone's ready, a player from each team tries to bounce the ball off the floor and into her goal. Each Bouncer gets 3 tries to score 1 point and then rebounds the ball and hands it to the next player.

4 The team with the most points wins.

Other Ways to Play

Time it: Play a 1-minute speed round.

Bounce, Roll, Toss

What You Do

1. Players divide into pairs. Each pair is a team. One player from each team stands on each side of the room. One player from each team holds a ball.

2. To play, each team moves the ball across the room and back to the first player from that team. The trick is that on the first cycle the ball must be bounced, on the second cycle the ball is rolled, and on the third cycle the ball is tossed. So, 1 round of play is made up of "bounce, bounce, roll, roll, toss, toss."

3. The first team to complete 5 rounds wins.

Number of Players: 4 or more
What You Need: 1 small, soft ball per team
Where to Play: in a room
The Point: move the ball

Bucket Brigade

What You Do

1 Players divide into 2 teams. Each team fills a bucket with packing peanuts and grabs 1 cup and 1 extra bucket. The teams line up single-file on opposite sides of the room so that the teams are facing one another.

2 Each team puts 1 empty bucket at one end of its line and the full bucket and cup at the other end.

3 Players count aloud from 1 to 3, and after "3" begin the race. Each player nearest a team's full bucket dips the cup in the peanuts and passes the cup down the line to the other end. The last player dumps the contents and passes the empty cup back.

Number of Players: 6 or more
What You Need: 4 buckets, 2 plastic cups, lots of packing peanuts
Where to Play: in a room
The Point: use teamwork to win

4 The first team to move all its peanuts to the empty bucket wins.

Busy Brooms

What You Do

1 The players stand on one side of the room. This is Start. Players stand a few feet away from one another, and each player gets 1 broom and 1 orange and places the orange nearby on the floor.

2 When everyone is ready, the players race to push their oranges to the opposite wall using only their brooms. After touching the opposite wall with the orange, each player turns and sweeps it back to Start.

3 Any player whose orange leaves the ground (such as from being hit or kicked) is Out. The first player to push an orange back to Start wins.

Number of Players: 2 or more
What You Need: 1 broom per player, 1 orange per player
Where to Play: in a room
The Point: sweep past opponents

Centipede Races

What You Do

1 Players agree on a Finish Line across the middle of the room, or mark one with string. Players then divide into teams.

2 The teams stand side by side on one end of the room in two single-file lines, so they resemble 2 Centipedes facing the Finish Line. The player at the front of each Centipede holds a balloon.

Number of Players: 6 or more
What You Need: 1 balloon per team
Where to Play: in a room or hallway
The Point: cross the finish

3 To begin the race, each first player lifts the balloon overhead and hands it back to the second player. Each second player passes the balloon between his legs to the third player. Players on both teams alternate over-head and between-the-legs passes until the balloon reaches the last player in the line.

4 The last player races to the front of his Centipede, and the passing starts again. So, it's as if the Centipede has taken a step forward. The first Centipede to get all its players across the Finish Line wins.

Cup Crossing

What You Do

1 Players cut 2 lengths of string about 10 feet long. Players use the pencil to poke a hole in the bottom of each cup, and then thread 1 cup through each length of string.

2 Players tie each lengths of string no higher than eye level, side by side (with about 2 feet between them) across the room. (Players could tie the string to chairs instead.) The open sides of the cups must face the same direction.

3 To begin the race, each player lines up at the open side of a cup and blows in the cup to push it along the string, all the way to the other side.

4 The first player to blow a cup to the end wins.

Number of Players: 2

What You Need: string, scissors, tape (optional), pencil, 2 small paper cups, 2 chairs (optional)

Where to Play: in a room

The Point: use your lungpower

Other Ways to Play

Teams: The first player who blows the cup all the way to the other side then slides the cup back to Start and a teammate takes a turn. Or, a player who runs out of breath can ask for help and have a teammate take over.

Diddly-Squat Races

What You Do

1. Players pair up and select a racecourse and a Finish Line. Then each player squats and tucks his arms behind his thighs.

2. Teammates line up back-to-back and place a scrap of paper between them. When everyone is ready, the teams race by crab walking to the finish line without dropping the paper.

3. The first team to finish wins.

Number of Players: 4 or more
What You Need: 1 scrap of paper per team
Where to Play: in a carpeted room
The Point: pair up and squat down

Other Ways to Play

More stuffing: Replace the piece of paper with a stuffed toy or a ball. (Nothing sharp!)

Didn't-Know-It Poet

What You Do

1. Players line up against a wall on one end of the hallway. Players will walk to the opposite end of the hallway to finish the race. The space between Start and Finish is the Poetry Field.

2. To begin the game, 1 player finishes the phrase, "When I was a ___," creating a rhyme to go with the word chosen to fill in the blank. For instance, "When I was a kid, you wouldn't believe what I did." Saying the entire verse aloud makes that player a Poet, and the Poet begins walking across the Poetry Field.

3. As quickly as possible, a different player must recite the first part and say a new rhyme for the second part. For instance, "When I was a kid, I called myself Sid." As soon as the rhyming word is said, the Poet in the Poetry Field stops moving. At the same time, the new Poet begins walking.

Number of Players: 3 or more
What You Need: nothing
Where to Play: in a hallway
The Point: out-verse other Poets

4. The new Poet walks until another player (or Poet) creates the next verse. If a player messes up a rhyme, someone else gets a turn.

5. The first Poet to reach the opposite wall wins.

Other Ways to Play

Start again: Remember to change the word used to complete, "When I was a ___" for each game. Don't start with anything too hard, such as "When I was a sausage."

Fast Food Delivery

Number of Players: 3 or more
What You Need: lots of balloons, a tray
Where to Play: in a room
The Point: finish the delivery

What You Do

1. Players divide into 2 teams. Each team gets a tray and half of the balloons. Players blow up the balloons.

2. Both teams pile their balloons on one end of the room, in separate piles. This is the Start. The opposite end of the room will be the Finish.

3. To play, teams carry 1 balloon at a time on the tray to the Finish line. If a balloon drops, the player has to stop, lay the tray on the floor, and pick up the balloon before picking up the tray and continuing the race. At the Finish, a player sets the tray on the floor, places the balloon in a pile, and then race back to Start to give a team-mate a turn.

4. The first team to move all its balloons to the Finish wins.

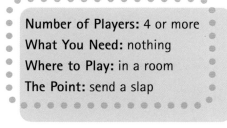

Number of Players: 4 or more
What You Need: nothing
Where to Play: in a room
The Point: send a slap

Hand Slap

What You Do

1. Players divide into 2 teams. If there are an odd number of players, let 1 person be the Referee.

2. Each team sits in a single-file row, facing the other team. Agree on one side of the room, to the right or left, to be Start.

3. To play, the player nearest the Start of each team's row (at the end) uses 1 hand to slap the hand of the next player. That player passes it on, down the row, and then back to Start.

4. Pass right-hand slaps in the right hand, and left-hand slaps in the left hand.

5. The first team to send a slap in both directions (down and back up its row) wins.

Other Ways to Play

Backhand: Have players slap the backs of their hands, instead of the palms.

Go behind: Pass the slaps behind the back. Players will have to twist and turn.

Hoop Hop........

What You Do

1 The players each place a hoop against a wall and then line up against the opposite wall.

2 To begin the game, players start hopping toward their hoops as quickly as possible. When they reach their hoops, players hop inside them, slide them up and over, and put the hoop back on the floor.

3 Then the players turn and hop back to Start. The first to finish wins. The first player to reach Start wins.

Other Ways to Play

Backward: Players hop backward—either throughout the game or just on the race back from the hoop.
Hula: After hopping into the hoops, players must circle the hoops around their waist or hips (by swinging their hips) 3 times before sliding the hoop up and over.

Number of Players: 2 or more
What You Need: 1 hula hoop per player
Where to Play: in a room
The Point: move through hoops

Hoop Race

Number of Players: 8 or more
What You Need: 2 hula hoops
Where to Play: in a room
The Point: pass the hoop

What You Do

1 Players divide into 2 teams. Each team grabs a hoop and the teams line up single-file on opposite sides of the room.

2 The teammates hold hands and a player on one end of each team's line holds the hoop in a free hand.

3 To begin the race, the teams count aloud together from 1 to 3. After saying, "3," each team passes the hoop from one end to the other, without letting go of anyone's hands. (So, players will need to wiggle the hoop over their heads and lift their legs to step through the hoop.)

4 The first team to get the hoop to the free hand of its player on the opposite end of the chain of players wins.

If the Shoe Fits

Number of Players: 2 or more
What You Need: multiple pairs of shoes in various sizes and styles, your own shoes
Where to Play: in a carpeted room
The Point: complete a lap

What You Do

1 Pile the extra shoes at one end of the room. Mix them up so that the mates aren't side by side.

2 Then the players take off their own shoes, add them to the pile, and players line up on the opposite side of the room.

3 When everyone's ready, the players race to pick 2 unmatched shoes and slip them on. Then the players race to the other end of the room, and then back to the shoe pile.

4 The first player to complete a lap wins.

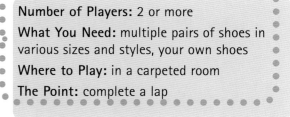

Jump-Hop-Skip

> **Number of Players:** 4 or more
> **What You Need:** nothing
> **Where to Play:** in a big carpeted room
> **The Point:** root-on your teammates

What You Do

1. The players divide into 2 teams. Both teams stand on one side of the room and agree on a Finish Line on the opposite side of the room.

2. When the game begins, a player from each team races to the Finish Line, crosses it, and then returns to Start so the next teammate can complete a lap. Here's the trick: Players must jump, hop, and then skip—and repeat.

3. Teammates help their players keep track by hollering, "Jump," "Hop," or "Skip" at the right time. Players who mess up walk quickly back to Start and begin again.

4. The first team that completes the circuit wins.

Other Ways to Play

Call out: Have a Referee randomly call out "Jump," "Hop," or "Skip." Players keep moving as directed until they get a new order from the Ref.

Jump Rope Relay

> **Number of Players:** 4 or more
> **What You Need:** 1 jump rope per team
> **Where to Play:** in a carpeted room without a ceiling fan
> **The Point:** jump rope race

What You Do

1. The players divide into 2 teams. Both teams stand on one side of the room. That location is Start. Players agree on a Finish Line on the opposite side of the room.

2. When the race begins, a player from each team jumps rope to the opposite side of the room, turns at the Finish Line, and returns to Start. The next player from each team takes the jump rope and completes the same circuit.

3. The first team to complete the circuit wins.

Other Ways to Play

Alternate feet: Players alternate which foot they land on with each jump.
Rope twist: Players cross their arms to twist the rope on every other jump.

Obstacle Course

What You Do

1 Players lay out this course in a loop around the room and take turns racing through the course while being timed. Players get 1 second of penalty added to their times for messing up on the obstacle course.

2 Lay the brooms on the floor to make a balance beam. At the end of the balance beam lay down the stepstool on its side. At the end of the stepstool set up the soda bottles in a slalom course pattern, not so close that a player can't walk between them, but close enough that a player would knock them down if going too fast.

3 At the end of the slalom course, place the hula hoop on the floor. On the other side of the hoop, lay down 2 pieces of newspaper. Leave at least 5 feet clear before the Finish Line. Use string to mark the Finish Line.

4 To race, players take turns timing each other as they complete the following route: walk across the balance beam without touching the floor or falling; walk through the stepstool without tripping; walk backwards between and around the soda bottles without knocking any over; step into the hoop; lift it up over the head; lay it back on the floor; pick up the newspaper and put down 1 piece for each foot for each step. (So, the player will have to balance on 1 foot while putting down paper for the next step.) Players walk this way across the Finish Line. Both feet have to be across the Finish Line to end the time.

5 After every player has run the race, the winner is the player who completed the course in the least time (including penalty seconds).

Number of Players: 3 or more
What You Need: timer, broom, stepstool, 4 or more empty soda bottles, hula hoop, 2 pages of newspaper, string (optional)
Where to Play: in a large room (or more than 1 room)
The Point: get over the obstacles

Old Hat

Number of Players: 6 or more
What You Need: 1 large serving spoon per player, 1 hat per player
Where to Play: in a room
The Point: use spoons like hands

What You Do

1 The players divide into 2 teams. Each team lines up in a single-file row in the middle of the room, and sits facing the other team.

2 Each player gets a serving spoon and holds it in 1 hand. The other hand cannot touch the serving spoon or the hat during play.

3 Next to each team, pile 1 hat per teammate. When play begins, each team picks up and passes a hat down its row, using only the spoons. When the hat reaches the end of the row, the player on the end must put on the hat, and then

quickly crawl to the start of the row. (The player can use hands to put on the hat.)

4 Once seated at the start of the row, the player wearing a hat passes the second (new) hat down the row. Continue until all the hats are passed and then worn.

5 If a hat is dropped, the player who was trying to pass it must pick it up with a spoon and put it back in play.

6 The first team whose players all have hats on wins.

Other Ways to Play

Switch: Players use a non-dominant hand, so right-handed players use their left hands, and left-handed players use their right hands.

Out of Breath

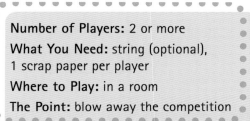

Number of Players: 2 or more
What You Need: string (optional), 1 scrap paper per player
Where to Play: in a room
The Point: blow away the competition

What You Do

1 Players kneel on the floor in a row, all facing the same direction. This is the Start line.

2 Players pick a spot about 5 feet in front of them and mark a Finish line with string, if necessary.

3 Each player wads up a scrap of paper, making a ball and placing it at the Start line. The smaller the ball, the easier the game is.

4 When the race begins, players blow on the paper balls, pushing the balls toward the Finish Line.

5 The first player to finish wins.

Other Ways to Play

Use a straw: Have each player blow through a straw. This will cut down on the amount of accidental spit sprayed on other players.

Popcorn Push

What You Do

1 Players make a racecourse that's about 5 feet long and mark Start and Finish lines.

2 Then players line up at the Start with a kernel of popped corn each and kneel at least 2 feet apart, to avoid bumping heads.

3 Players crawl as they push the popped corn with their noses to the Finish Line.

4 The player who moves a kernel of popped corn across the Finish Line first wins.

Quick Fingers

Number of Players: 6 or more
What You Need: 2 pieces of rope of equal length
Where to Play: anywhere
The Point: race to untie the knots first

What You Do

1 Players divide into 2 teams. Each team gets 1 length of rope and ties knots in it, letting each player tie a knot. (Players tie any kind of knot.)

2 When both teams are ready, they switch ropes and rush to untie the knots. Each player unties a knot.

3 The first team to untie all the knots wins.

Slow Down

Number of Players: 2 or more
What You Need: a timer
Where to Play: in a room
The Point: run a closed-eye race

What You Do

1 Players line up on one side of the room and agree on a Finish Line on the opposite side of the room.

2 One player sets the timer for 1 minute and says, "Go!" Each player closes both eyes and begins moving as slowly as possible to the Finish Line. Players must be moving constantly.

3 No one can peek at other players or the timer. (If someone peeks, pick a Referee to watch the race, and start again.)

4 The winner is the last to finish before the timer dings.

Spare Change Charge

What You Do

1 Players line up against a wall and put a coin on their foreheads (1 coin per player). Players lean their heads back just enough so the coin doesn't fall. (No hands!)

2 To begin the game, players race to the opposite wall, balancing the coins.

Number of Players: 2 or more
What You Need: 1 coin per player
Where to Play: in a room
The Point: balance a coin

3 If a coin falls, that player must stop, pick up the coin, balance it again, and then resume the race.

4 The first player to reach the opposite wall wins.

Swim Contest

What You Do

1. One player is the Referee. The other players are Swimmers.

2. Swimmers lay out their rafts on the floor. Swimmers need enough room to dog paddle with their feet and kick their legs without hitting anyone else. The Referee should be able to see all the Swimmers at once.

3. When everyone is ready, the Referee begins the game by blowing the whistle or saying, "On your mark, get set, go!" Swimmers begin swimming, picking up their arms and legs and making swimming motions.

Number of Players: 4 or more
What You Need: 1 inflatable raft per player (or beach towels), a whistle (optional)
Where to Play: in a room
The Point: "swim" the furthest

4. If a Swimmer touches the floor, the Swimmer is out of the game. The Swimmer who can swim for the longest time wins.

Toe to Toe

What You Do

1. Players take off their shoes and socks, and pair up on one side of the room. If there's an extra player, let that person be the Referee.

2. Each pair of players sits on the floor toe to toe. Legs can be bent or straight. The teams line up back to back, so all the teams are in one line.*

3. Agree on a Finish Line on the opposite side of the room. Mark this with a string, if necessary.

4. When the race begins, teams roll toward the Finish Line. If a pair's toes stop touching, the team has to move back to Start and begin again.

5. The first team to cross the Finish Line—toes still touching—wins.

Number of Players: 4 or more
What You Need: stopwatch or watch with a second hand (optional), string (optional)
Where to Play: in a carpeted room
The Point: make the fastest toe-to-toe roll

*If the room is too small to have more than one team race at a time, time each team as it takes a turn rolling to the Finish Line. Compare the results to see who wins.

Other Ways to Play

Hand to hand: Instead of touching toes, try playing the game holding hands.

Tricky Hand-Off

What You Do

1. Players divide into 2 teams. If there's an extra player, let that person be the Referee.

2. Each team's players sit side by side in a single-file row. The teams face one another.

3. Each team piles 3 marbles to the left (at the end of its row) and 3 coins to the right (at the other end of its row).

4. To play, the teams pass each object one at a time, from one player to another, to the end of the row. The tricky part is remembering which hand to use for which object. Marbles move to the right and are passed with the right hand. Coins move to the left and are passed with the left hand.

Number of Players: 6 or more
What You Need: 3 marbles and 3 coins per team
Where to Play: in a room or hallway
The Point: pass objects in 2 directions

5. Players can't hold more than one object in one hand. Players also can't use the wrong hand to pass an object. The penalty for breaking either rule is that the object goes back to Start.

6. A team wins by moving all its marbles and coins to the opposite ends first.

BALL GAMES

Who knew you could play ball in the house?

500

What You Do

1 One player is the Thrower. The other players are Catchers. The Thrower and Catchers stands on opposite sides of the room.

2 The Thrower tosses the rolled-up sock toward the Catchers and says a number between 50 and 500. That's how many points a Catcher earns for catching it—or loses for trying to catch but missing! (Catchers should call out, "Mine!" to avoid bumping into each other.)

3 The first Catcher to earn 500 points wins and is the new Thrower.

Number of Players: 3 or more
What You Need: rolled-up sock
Where to Play: in a large room
The Point: throw and catch for points

Number of Players: 3 or more
What You Need: string (optional), 1 baseball cap per player, 1 small ball
Where to Play: against a wall
The Point: earn the lowest score

Bad Aim Is Good Aim

What You Do

1 Players place their caps upside down in front of the wall. The nearer the caps are to one another, the better. The goal is to get the lowest score. Players avoid earning points by getting the ball in an opponent's cap. Missing entirely earns 1 point. Landing in your own hat earns 2 points.

2 Players agree on a Throw Line, or mark a Throw Line with the string. Players must stand behind this line to throw. With everyone playing at the same time, players toss or bounce their balls toward the caps. Players keep their own scores.

3 After a set time or a set number of points, the player with the fewest points wins.

Bocce

Number of Players: 3 or more
What You Need: rolled-up sock, 1 paper or plastic plate per player
Where to Play: in a room
The Point: make the best toss

What You Do

1 Each player takes 1 plate and marks it with initials or a doodle—something to distinguish it from the other plates.

2 A player starts the game by tossing the rolled-up sock to the other end of the room. It doesn't matter where it lands, so long as there is space around it for the paper plates to land.

3 Each player takes a turn tossing his plate at the rolled-up sock. After each player has had a turn, the player whose plate landed on or nearest the sock wins the round and earns a point.

4 The first player to earn 11 points wins.

Other Ways to Play

Double up: Give each player 2 plates to toss per turn.

Bop

Number of Players: 2
What You Need: 1 balloon
Where to Play: in a room or hallway
The Point: keep the balloon afloat

What You Do

1 The players stand side by side and link elbows. One player holds a balloon in the hand of the free (unlinked) arm.

2 When the game begins, the players bop the balloon back and forth in the air, using only their free hands.

3 Players count how many passes they complete before the balloon touches the floor.

Bowling Bridges

What You Do

1. Players divide into 2 teams. The teams line up on opposite sides of the room so teammates stand side by side and face the other team. Teammates stand no less than 1 foot apart and with their feet spread no less than the width of the ball.

2. To play, teams take turns rolling the ball at one another. Players aren't allowed to move while a ball is being rolled. If the ball goes between the legs of an player, that player is out of the game.

3. The first team to eliminate everyone on the other team wins.

Number of Players: 6 or more
What You Need: 1 small ball
Where to Play: in a room
The Point: eliminate opponents

Number of Players: 2 or more
What You Need: 1 rolled-up sock, 1 broom per player, 2 hand towels (optional)
Where to Play: on a hard floor
The Point: score goals

Broom Hockey

What You Do

1. Players divide into 2 teams. Each player needs a broom. Each team needs a scoring goal, and the goals should be located at opposite ends of the room. (A hand towel makes a good goal.)

2. Teams line up in the middle of the room. Players from each team should have their backs to the goal they're protecting and be facing their scoring goal. One rolled-up sock is the puck.

3. To begin, a player tosses the puck straight up into the air. When it hits the floor, players begin trying to push the puck to their goal to score a point.

4. After a team scores, the other team gets 1 "free" chance to sweep the sock to a teammate or toward their scoring goal. (But the other team can block or intercept.)

5. The first team to score 11 points wins.

Foot Volleyball

What You Do

1. Players divide the playing area into a volleyball court with 2 equal-sized sides. Do this by tying the string across the area, about 1 foot off the floor. (Use 2 chairs, 1 on each side of the court.) The string line is the net.

2. Players remove their shoes and divide into 2 teams, with 1 team on each side of the net. Players sit on the floor and then lean back onto their hands, lifting up so that only their hands and feet touch the ground, as if crab walking.

3. To start, 1 team serves the ball by kicking the balloon over the net. If the other team kicks it into or below the net or lets it touch the ground, instead of hitting it back over the net, the team that served earns a point and gets to serve again. If the serving team messes up, the other team gets to serve and has a chance to earn points.

> **Number of Players:** 2 or more (even numbers work best)
>
> **What You Need:** a string or rope, a large inflated balloon
>
> **Where to Play:** in a room
>
> **The Point:** use your feet to score

4. Play until a team wins by earning 11 points.

Other Ways to Play

Play longer: Agree to play to the score of 15 or 21.

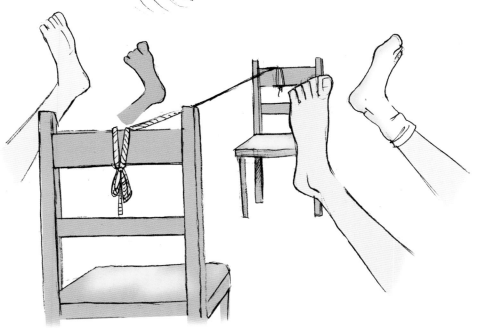

Golf Ball Billiards

Number of Players: 2 or more
What You Need: string, 10 golf balls, and 1 unsharpened pencil per player
Where to Play: on a hard floor
The Point: score 5 knock-outs

What You Do

1. Players make a circle on the floor with the string. The circle should be 3 feet in diameter. Players place 9 golf balls inside the circle.

2. Players use a colored golf ball (or mark a plain one) for the cue ball. Each player gets a pencil and decides in which order to play.

3. Players use the pencil like a real pool cue, sliding it along the hand to push the cue ball into a golf ball.

4. The goal is to knock as many golf balls out of the circle as possible. If a player knocks a ball out, he gets another turn, unless the cue ball is knocked out as well. A player can shoot until failing to knock a ball out of he circle.

5. Then the next player shoots. The player shoots from wherever the cue ball rolled at the end of the last player's turn. If the ball goes out of the circle, the next player can put it anywhere in the circle.

6. Whoever knocks 5 balls out of the circle first wins.

Other Ways to Play

One at a time: Take turns every time, regardless of whether or not a player knocked a ball out of the circle.

SMACK!

Hurling

What You Do

1. One player is the Hurler. The Hurler stands on one side of the room. The other players line up against the opposite wall. The closer together they stand, the better.

2. The Hurler throws the roll-up sock at the players—aiming below the knees. A player can jump straight up to avoid being hit, but a player can't take more than 1 step in any direction to avoid the sock.

3. A player hit by the sock is Out. The last player still in the game wins and becomes the new Hurler.

Number of Players: 4 or more
What You Need: a rolled-up sock
Where to Play: in a room, against a wall
The Point: dodge the sock

Number of Players: 2 to 5
What You Need: water, 9 empty plastic soda bottles with caps, rubber ball
Where to Play: in a hallway
The Point: don't hit Jack

Jack

What You Do

1. Players pour a little water into each bottle. This helps the bottles stand. Players place the bottles in a pyramid pattern. The middle bottle is Jack.

2. To play, a player kneels at least 10 feet away from the bottles. (The further away, the better.) The player rolls the ball into the bottles. A player who knocks down 1 or more of the bottles on a turn without hitting Jack earns 2 points for each bottle.

3. Players stand the bottles back up and give another player a turn. If, in a single turn, a player knocks over all 8 bottles without hitting Jack, that player earns a 10-point bonus (in addition to the 2 points scored for each bottle). Then it's the next player's turn.

4. A player who hits 1 or more bottles and the Jack must subtract 2 points from the score for every bottle knocked over (except the Jack). That player's turn is over.

5. The first player to score 20 points wins.

Knee Squeeze

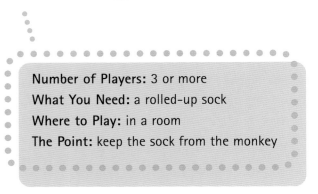

Number of Players: 2 or more
What You Need: 1 balloon per player
Where to Play: in a room
The Point: waddle to victory

What You Do

1 Players pace 1 balloon per player on the far side of the room, and then line up on the other side of the room. This is the Start.

2 Players count down from 3, and on "3" race to the far side of the room and pick up a balloon with their knees. No hands allowed.

3 Players race back to Start, waddling or walking with the balloon. No hopping. If a balloon falls to the floor, the player must pick it up again and continue the race.

4 The first player to return to Start wins.

Monkey in the Middle

Number of Players: 3 or more
What You Need: a rolled-up sock
Where to Play: in a room
The Point: keep the sock from the monkey

What You Do

1 One player is the Monkey. (The game is more fun if the Monkey isn't the shortest player.) The Monkey kneels in between the other players, who are also kneeling.

2 The other players toss the rolled-up sock and forth. The Monkey tries to grab it.

3 If the Monkey intercepts the sock, the player who threw it becomes the new Monkey.

Lower

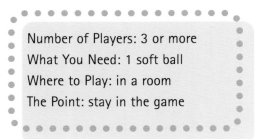

Number of Players: 3 or more
What You Need: 1 soft ball
Where to Play: in a room
The Point: stay in the game

What You Do

1 Players form a large circle. One player begins the game by tossing the ball to the player on the left. Players continue passing the ball this way around the circle.

2 If a player drops the ball, the others say, "Lower." That player must drop from both feet to both knees, but can still catch and toss the ball. A

player on his knees who drops the ball again must drop to his elbows. His next drop means that player has to lie flat on the floor! If a player who has dropped flat on the floor drops the ball again, that player is Out.

3 Play until there's only 1 person still in the game. That player wins.

Pinball

What You Do

1 One player is the pinball Jackpot. The Jackpot stands in the middle of the room. The other players sit on the floor in a circle around the Jackpot. They are the Flippers.

2 The Flippers in the circle spread their legs as wide as is comfortable and touch feet with the players on either side. The area inside the circle of feet is where the Pinball game happens.

3 The Flippers lean forward to rest their hands or arms on the floor. (If you're flexible, you may rest your whole arm on the floor.) Flippers will hit the ball with the hands or arms.

Number of Players: 5 or more
What You Need: a soft ball
Where to Play: on a floor
The Point: hit the Jackpot

4 The players count aloud together from 1 to 3, and then 1 of the Flippers starts the ball in play. The Flippers try to hit the Jackpot while Jackpot moves around to avoid being hit. The Jackpot can't leave the circle and ball can't leave the floor.

5 The Flipper who hits the Jackpot with the ball becomes the new Jackpot.

Round About

Number of Players: 3 or more
What You Need: a ball of any size
Where to Play: anywhere you can sit in a circle
The Point: pass the ball

What You Do

1 Players sit in a circle facing the center of the circle. One player is the Starter. The Starter begins passing the ball clockwise.

2 Each player must pass it exactly as the Starter passed it. For instance, the Starter might pass it by holding it with both hands.

3 After the ball is passed around once, the player to the left of the Starter must pass the ball in a new way. For instance, a player may pass it by balancing it on the back of the hand, or passing it under a leg.

4 If a player drops the ball or can't pass it, the player drops out of the circle. Each time a style of passing makes it all the way around the circle, the next person to the left begins a new style of passing.

5 The last remaining player wins. The winner starts the next game.

THiS iS EASY...

Socks of Fury

What You Do

1 Players stand or sit in a wide circle. One player begins the game by calling out another player's name and at the same time quickly tossing the rolled-up sock to that player.

2 The named player must catch the sock and name another player and throw it to that person as quickly as possible. Each name can only be used once. That means that once the sock has been tossed to each player, there is a system for who each player will always throw to.

3 When the sock has gone to each player at least once without anyone dropping it, add the second sock, and then the third.

Number of Players: 6 or more

What You Need: 3 rolled-up socks (preferably socks of different colors)

Where to Play: in a room

The Point: think faster than socks fly

Other Ways to Play

Hustle: Instead of throwing the sock to a player, call the player's name but throw the sock up into the air in the center, so the player has to hustle to catch it.

Step-Back Cup Catch

What You Do

1 Players line up in pairs and stand about 2 feet apart, facing one another. (If there are an odd number of players, have one player be the challenger to the winner of the first game.)

2 Players work as a team to toss the sock back and forth, catching it in their cups. Each time a player catches the sock the team takes a full step back. No small steps, unless young kids are playing. Let them take smaller steps.

3 Each team should count its steps out loud and keep track of them. Players who miss a catch must stay put.

4 The first team to take 5 steps wins.

Number of Players: 2 or more

What You Need: 1 rolled-up sock per team, 1 plastic cup for each player (large enough to hold the sock)

Where to Play: in a room or hallway

The Point: outcatch the other team

Other Ways to Play

More steps: When playing in a larger area, increase the number of steps required to win (10 instead of 5, for instance).

CARD GAMES

More fun than 52-Pickup. Guaranteed!

Anxiety ....

What You Do

1. Players sit in a circle. One player deals cards 1 at a time to each player until all the cards are dealt.

2. Players all flip over 1 card at the same time and toss it in the middle of the circle. If anyone flips over the Ace of Spades, all the other players tickle that player.

3. If no one flips over the Ace of Spades, keep playing until someone does. The longer the game lasts, the more anxious the players become.

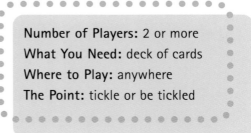

Number of Players: 2 or more
What You Need: deck of cards
Where to Play: anywhere
The Point: tickle or be tickled

Other Ways to Play

More: Assign actions to other cards. For example, the Jack of Hearts means the player gets bear hugs, or the 3 of Diamonds means the player's shoes are quickly removed by the other players.

Card Toss

What You Do

1. The players agree on a Toss Line. Then they pull out pages from the magazine and arrange the pages on the floor about 2 feet in front of the Toss line. The pages can't overlap.

2. The players divide the deck of cards equally, sit behind the Toss Line, and take turns tossing a card toward the pages.

3. When a card lands on a page, the player who tossed it gets 1 point. No other cards can earn points on that page. (So, if other cards land there, no points to those players.)

4. After all the cards have been tossed, the player with the most points wins.

Number of Players: 2 or more
What You Need: string, magazine you can destroy, deck of cards
Where to Play: in a room or hallway
The Point: throw cards for points

Other Ways to Play

Get tougher: Place the magazine pages further away. To make the game even harder, agree that a card must land completely on the magazine page in order to earn a point.

Be higher: Stand up to toss the cards.

Play faster: Have players line up side-by-side and toss at the same time. To keep track of who tossed which card, divide the cards by color, suit, or face value.

Crazy 8s

What You Do

1. One player is the Dealer and deals 7 cards to each player. Players hold the cards in their hands.

2. The Dealer stacks the rest of the deck face down in the middle of the table. The Dealer then turns over the top card from the deck and sets it beside the deck, creating a Discard pile.

3. The first player to the left of the Dealer starts. The aim is to discard 1 card per turn. But the discarded card must be the same as the face-up card, either in value (9, Jack) or suit (heart, spade, diamond, club).

Number of Players: 2 or more
What You Need: deck of cards
Where to Play: on a table or floor
The Point: empty your hand

4. If the player does not have a card to discard, the player draws 1 card from the deck. If that card cannot be discarded, the player keeps it, and the next player has a turn.

5. Eights are wild, so a player could discard an 8 on a turn, no matter the value or suit of the face-up card. The player who discards all cards first wins.

Even Stevens

What You Do

1. One player is the Dealer, and deals 7 cards to each player.

2. The Dealer places the rest of the deck face down on the table.

3. The opponent begins the game by placing 1 card face up on the table. This will be the Pile.

4. The Dealer must play a single card of the same value as the card laid in the Pile. This matching card is called an Even Steven.

5. If the Dealer has no Even Steven, the Dealer can't play any card, and picks up a card from the deck. It's the opponent's turn.

6. If the Dealer has an Even Steven and lays it down, it's now the opponent's turn to lay down another Even Steven, or pick up a card from the deck.

7. Whenever a player fails to lie out an Even Steven, the player must pick up 1 card from the deck, and the other player may lie out any new card face up on the Pile.

8. The first player to use up all the cards in his hand wins.

Guess What

What You Do

1. One player is the Dealer and deals 5 cards to each player. Players hold the 5 cards in their hands so no one else can see them.

2. The Dealer takes the top card from the deck and places that card facedown in front of the players. That card is the What.

3. Each player guesses which card What is, and then "bids" a card from her hand based on that guess. To bid, a player places just 1 of her cards face-up above or below the facedown card. Place a card above to say you think your card is of greater value. Place a card below to say it is of less value than the facedown card.

4. When every player has made 1 bid, the Dealer turns over the What to reveal it. The Dealer determines who won their bid. Those players get to take their Winning Card and set it aside as 1 point. Players who lost their bids lose those cards; the cards go to the bottom of the deck along with the What.

5. For each round, the Dealer places new What facedown and players bid 1 card. When all five rounds have been played, the player with the most points wins.

Hat Trick

What You Do

1. Players divide the cards equally among themselves and set the hat flat on the floor against the wall.

2. Players agree on a Toss Line and take turns flipping the cards against the wall, standing, sitting or squatting behind the Toss Line.

3. A player earns 1 point for each successful bank shot. No points for tossing the card directly into the hat. Scoring 3 times in a row is a Hat Trick; that player earns 3 extra points.

4. After all the cards are tossed, the player with the most points wins.

Other Ways to Play

Three-point shots: Create a second Toss Line, further away, from which players can make 3-point shots.

Heartbreaker

What You Do

1 One player deals a card to each player, clockwise, until all the cards are handed out.

2 Players hold the cards in their hands and sort out all the pairs. Pairs are laid on the table. Hearts can be laid as pairs, but anyone holding a single heart is a Heartbreaker. (So if you have a single heart, keep it secret.)

3 To begin the game, the player to the left of the dealer pulls 1 card (any card) from the hand of any one of the players. If that card makes a pair with a card in the player's hand, the player lays the pair on the table. Otherwise, the card is held.

> **Number of Players:** 2 or more
> **What You Need:** deck of cards
> **Where to Play:** on a table or floor
> **The Point:** avoid Heartbreakers

4 Play continues around the table, with each player getting 1 chance to pick a card per turn.

5 If a player picks a Heartbreaker and can't immediately use it to make a pair, that player who picked it forfeits all pairs. He gives them to the player who held the Heartbreaker. The unlucky player keeps the Heartbreaker.

6 The player with the most pairs at game's end wins.

House of Cards

> **Number of Players:** 2 or more
> **What You Need:** deck of cards
> **Where to Play:** on a table or floor
> **The Point:** construct a House of Cards

What You Do

1 One player starts the game by trying to build a structure at the center of the table using no more than 4 cards from the deck.

2 Players take turns using up to 4 cards to start or add onto the structure.

3 The player who knocks down the House of Cards has to clean up the cards and starts the new House.

Instant Win

What You Do

1 One player shuffles the deck. The player to the left cuts the deck, dividing the cards into 2 half stacks and placing the lower half on top.

2 The player who cut the deck then turns over the top card. If it's a Jack, the player wins.

3 Play continues with each player having a turn to cut the deck and turn over the new top card.

4 The first player to turn over a Jack wins.

Number of Players: 2 or more
What You Need: deck of cards
Where to Play: anywhere
The Point: find a Jack

Number of Players: 2 or more
What You Need: deck of cards
Where to Play: on a table or floor
The Point: collect the most pairs

Lightning Pairs

What You Do

1 One player deals a card to each player, clockwise, until all the cards are handed out.

2 Play begins immediately, as players hold the cards in their hands and sort out all the pairs. Pairs are laid face up on the table, according to the following rule: only 1 kind of pair can be laid out. So, the first player to lay out a pair of 2s is the only player who can lay out a pair of 2s, etc. Be quick!

3 After players lay out the allowed pairs, the player to the left of the dealer pulls 1 card (any card) from the hand of any one of the players. If that card makes an original pair with a card in the player's hand, the player lays the pair on the table.

4 Play continues once around the table, with each player getting just one chance to pick a card per turn.

5 At the end of 1 round, the player with the most pairs wins.

Matches

Number of Players: 2 or more
What You Need: deck of cards
Where to Play: on a table or floor
The Point: make the most matches

What You Do

1   One player is the Dealer and deals 8 cards to the center of the table, placing them face up. Then the Dealer deals 4 cards to each player. The extra cards are set aside, face down.

2   Players look at their cards, and then turn them face up. The player to the left of the Dealer begins play.

3   On each turn a player can remove a card from the center, but only if 1 of her cards matches it in suit or value. For instance, if there's a 5 of clubs in the center, a player holding any club or any 5 could pick the 5 of clubs as a match. The player who removes a card pairs it with the "match" and lays them in a pile. A player who can't make a match must put a card in the center of the table. Play continues to the left.

4   When all players have used or handed out their cards, the player with the most matches wins.

Number of Players: 2 or more
What You Need: deck of cards
Where to Play: tabletop or flat surface
The Point: reunite each set of quadruplets

Quadruplets

What You Do

1   One player deals a card to each player, clockwise, until all the cards are handed out.

2   Players look at their cards, but don't show them to anyone. Players lay their cards face down on the table.

3   Players want to collect as many sets of 4 of a kind as they can. When a player has 4 of a kind, the player turns them face up.

4   Taking turns and moving clockwise, each player asks any one of the other players for exactly the card wanted. (If a player has an Ace, that player will want all the Aces, but can only ask for 1 at a time, such as the Ace of Hearts.)

5   If the player asked has the card, that player has to hand it over. Then the next player takes a turn.

6   Players must remember to turn over any 4-of-a-kind collection as soon as possible. Any facedown cards are fair game for other players to request.

7   The game ends when all of the quadruplets have been reunited and no one has any cards left.

Royalty...........................

Number of Players: 2 or more
What You Need: deck of cards
Where to Play: on a table or floor
The Point: act out characters

What You Do

1. One player deals a card to each player until all the cards are handed out. Players can't look at their cards.

2. The player to the left of the Dealer quickly lays out 1 card faceup, creating a pile. The next player lays a card on the pile and so on, so each player is laying out a card 1 at a time.

3. As soon as anyone sees a royalty card (King, Queen, or Jack), the first player to act out the royal character gets the royalty card and all the cards under it. Winning a King requires that a player be the first to say, "The King says it is so, and so it is so." Winning a Queen requires that

the player be the first to kiss the air to the right and left, as if kissing each cheek of a friend. A player must be the first to stand and salute in order to win a Jack.

4. That winning player puts the cards in her hand and starts a new pile, laying down the first card.

5. The player who has all the cards at game's end wins.

Subtraction War

Number of Players: 2 or more
What You Need: deck of cards
Where to Play: on a table or floor
The Point: use math to win cards

What You Do

1 One player deals a card to each player until all the cards are handed out.

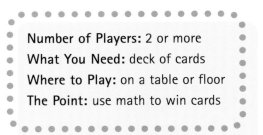

PLAYER #1

$10 - 10 = 0$

PLAYER #2 WINS

$4 - 2 = 2$

2 To begin the game, all players lay out 2 cards, face up, at the same time. Players subtract their own lower card from their higher card. (Every card above 10 is worth 10 points.) The player with the highest sum wins the round and takes all the cards played.

3 The player who has all the cards at game's end wins.

Trap

Number of Players: 3 to 6
What You Need: deck of cards
Where to Play: on a table or floor
The Point: trap your opponents

What You Do

1 The Dealer distributes an even number of cards to the players. If there are any extra cards, set them aside face down.

2 The player to the left of the Dealer lays out 1 card face up. Any card.

3 The next player to the left can Trap the card by placing the next lower and higher cards on either side. To trap a 6, for instance, a player would need to surround it with a 5 and a 7. After trapping a card, the Trapper scoops up all 3 cards and stacks them nearby. This stack counts as 1 point.

4 If the player can't Trap the card, the player must lay out another card elsewhere on the table. Play continues moving clockwise and players can play off of any cards on the table. That means players can Trap their own cards.

5 When all the cards have been laid on the table once, the player with the most Traps wins.

Triplet

What You Do

1. The Dealer distributes an even number of cards to the players. If there are any extra cards, set them aside face down.

2. The player to the left of the Dealer lays out 1 card face up.

3. The next player to the left can create a Triplet using the card by laying out 2 cards of the same value or suit from his hand. So, there could be a Triplet made up of diamonds, or a Triplet made up of Kings.

4. If the next player can't make a Triplet using the card on the table, the player must lay out 1 card elsewhere on the table.

5. Play continues moving clockwise. Players can play off any card on the table.

6. The first player to use all the cards in her hand wins.

Number of Players: 3 or more
What You Need: deck of cards
Where to Play: on a table or floor
The Point: empty your hand of cards

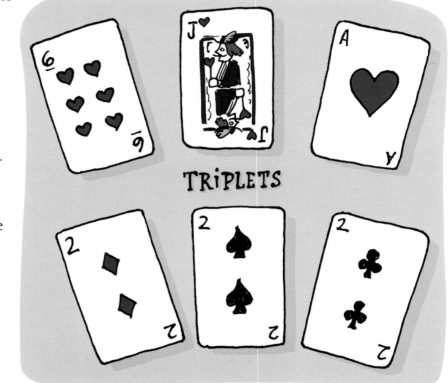

TRIPLETS

MARBLES, COINS & DICE

Shoot, flip, toss, and roll.

Basic Marbles

What You Do

1. Players make a circle on the floor with the dental floss. It should be about 2 to 3 feet wide. Players decide which order to play in.

2. Each player puts the same number of marbles into the center of the circle, saving a taw, or shooter marble. The taw is usually slighter larger and heavier than the other marbles. Players use it to knock the other marbles out of the circle.

3. To shoot a taw, a player places it outside of the circle, holds it as shown above, and shoots it toward the marbles in the middle.

4. A player keeps any marbles knocked out of the circle. The player continues to shoot until failing to knock any marbles out of the circle. The player leaves the taw where it is, unless it rolled outside of the circle.

5. If a player hits another player's taw, the shooter gets all the marbles that that player has collected so far.

6. After all the marbles have been knocked out of the circle, the player with the most marbles wins.

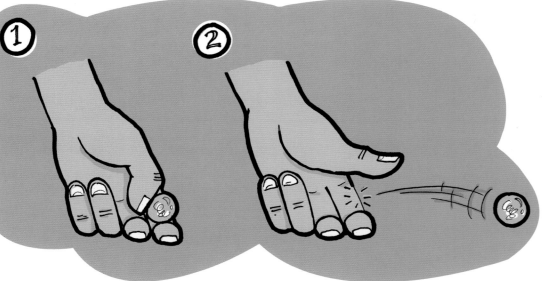

Bull's Eye

What You Do

1. Players make a 1-foot-wide circle on the floor with the dental floss. Players put 1 marble for each player into the center of the circle.

2. Players take turns standing over the circle and dropping a marble into it. Players must drop the marble from eye level.

3. If a player's marble knocks any other marble out of the ring, that player gets to keep it. After each turn, players leave their marbles where they are. Players use a new marble for every turn.

4. When all the marbles have been knocked out of the circle, players count their marbles. The player with the most marbles wins.

Number of Players: 2 or more
What You Need: dental floss or very thin string, marbles
Where to Play: on a hard floor
The Point: make bomber shots

Coin Flip

What You Do

1. Draw a target on the paper. Place the target on a flat surface.

2. Mark a line with the string at least 1 foot away from the target. This is the Flip Line.

3. Players take turns flipping the coins into the target. (Flip a coin by balancing it on your thumb and then flicking the end of your thumb with your index finger.) Players earn the number of points in the area of the target in which their coin lands.

4. The first player to score 10 points wins.

Number of Players: 2 or more
What You Need: piece of paper, pencil, string 1 coin for each player
Where to Play: on any flat surface
The Point: hit the target

Dobblers

What You Do

1 Players make 1 straight line of marbles. The marbles should each be far enough apart for 2 marbles to pass between them. Players decide which order to play in and kneel at the Shooting Line.

2 One player shoots a taw or shooter marble, at the marbles. The taw is usually slighter larger and heavier than the other marbles. Any marble that the taw hits, the player gets to keep. Whether a player knocks into any marbles or not, the turn is over.

3 Players leave their taws where they are at the end of the turn. Players have to shoot from wherever their taw is on the next turn.

4 If a player hits someone else's taw, that player must add a marble to the line of marbles.

5 When all the marbles are gone, the player with the most marbles wins.

Number of Players: 2 or more
What You Need: dental floss or very thin string, marbles
Where to Play: on a hard floor
The Point: stay in the right circles

Number of Players: 2 or more
What You Need: marbles
Where to Play: on a hard floor
The Point: hit the lines of marbles

Double Ring

What You Do

1 Players "draw" a circle on the floor with the dental floss. It should be about 2 to 3 feet wide. Players "draw" another smaller circle inside that circle. The smaller circle should be about 6 inches across.

2 Players place the marbles in the inner circle. Players take turns shooting their taws from the outer circle.

3 A player must knock the marbles out of both circles, and the taw must be in the outer circle at the end of the turn. A player keeps the marbles he knocked out. If the taw ends up in the inner circle, the player must put all the marbles just knocked out of the circle back into the inner circle.

Fivestones

What You Do

1 One player starts by throwing 5 stones into the air with one hand. The player tries to catch them on the back of that same hand before they hit the floor.

2 If the player doesn't catch any of the stones on the back of the hand, it's the next player's turn. If the player catches some of the stones, the player throws them into the air again, and catches them in the palm of that hand.

3 The player keeps 1 of the stones in the throwing hand and tosses all of the other stones on the floor.

4 The player throws the stone in the hand into the air. The player must pick up 1 stone off the floor with that same hand, and then catch the stone thrown in the air. If the player makes it, the player goes again until all the stones have been picked up. The player must use the same hand for everything.

5 Once a player has picked up all of the stones, the player throws 4 of them down again. Then the player throws the 1 remaining stone into the air, picks up 2 of the other stones, and catches the 1 in the air. Next time, the player picks up the last 2 stones.

6 On the next round, the players pick up 3 of the stones at once, and on the final round, they pick up all of the stones at one time.

Number of Players: 2 or more
What You Need: 5 stones (or dried beans)
Where to Play: anywhere you can sit in a circle on the floor
The Point: catch as many stones as possible

7 If at any point a player doesn't pick up all the stones in 1 turn, or doesn't catch the stone before it falls, the next player gets to go.

8 The first player to make it all the way through the rounds wins.

Hot or Cold

What You Do

1. One player is the Hider and the others are all Searchers. One player hides the small object while the other players close their eyes or leave the room. Putting it inside something unexpected is always a good idea (such as putting a penny in a book).

2. When the object is hidden, the Searchers begin looking for it. The Hider gives hints by saying, "you are getting warmer" if a Searcher is getting near the object, and "you are getting colder" if a Searcher is moving away from the object.

3. A player wins by finding the object. That player becomes the Hider.

Number of Players: 2 or more
What You Need: coin or other small object
Where to Play: anywhere
The Point: find the hidden object

Luck

Number of Players: 2 or more
What You Need: 1 die per player (a die is half of a pair of dice)
Where to Play: anywhere
The Point: make lucky rolls to win

What You Do

1. Each player gets 1 die. Players take turns rolling a die, 1 roll per turn.

2. Players must roll 1, 2, 3, 4, 5, and 6 in order. So, if the first player rolls a 1 on the first try, in the next roll that player wants a 2. If that player's next roll is not a 2, the player keeps trying with each turn to roll a 2 before moving on to 3, etc.

3. The first player to roll 1 through 6 in order wins.

Money Knock Down

Number of Players: 3 or more
What You Need: 10 or more empty aluminum cans, coins
Where to Play: in a room
The Point: flick coins at cans for points

What You Do

1. Players stack the cans on the floor in any way they like, so long as the stack stands on its own. (The cans should be clean so the floor doesn't get dirty or stained.)

2. Players take turns flicking a coin at the cans. Players get a point for each can knocked down, or 10 points for knocking down all the cans with 1 flick.

3. Play until all the cans are down. The player with the most points wins.

Monkey Feet

What You Do

1. Players remove their socks and shoes and stand on one side of the room. This is the Start line. Players agree on a Finish line on the opposite side of the room.

2. Each barefoot player gets 1 coin and lays it on the floor. Count down from 3 to start the game. Then each player must pick up the coin using only 1 foot, and move the coin to the Finish line.

3. Ways to pick up a coin include pressing into the coin with the fleshy ball of the foot (easiest on hard floors) and grabbing the coin between two toes (easiest on carpeted floors).

4. Players can drop coins and pick them up again, but if the coin rolls forward it must be taken back to where the player's foot was when the coin dropped.

5. The first player to reach the Finish line with a coin "in foot" wins.

> **Number of Players:** 2 or more
> **What You Need:** 1 coin per player (use the same kind of coin for everyone)
> **Where to Play:** in a room
> **The Point:** use your feet like hands

Other Ways to Play

More monkeying: All players sit on the floor. Instead of picking up a coin with 1 foot, players pick up and carry the coin between both feet, scooting along the floor by pushing with their hands.

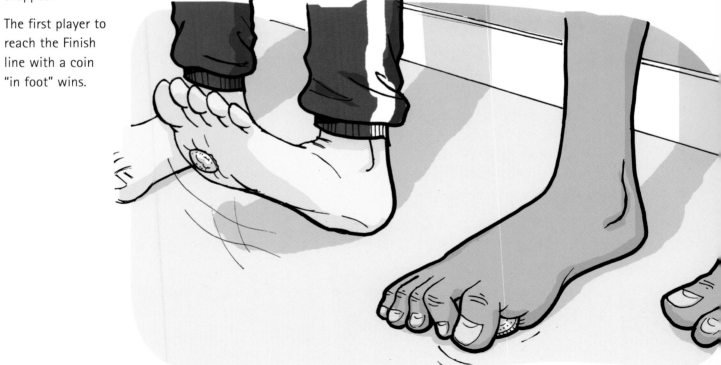

Pyramid Marbles

Number of Players: 2 or more
What You Need: dental floss and marbles
Where to Play: on a hard floor
The Point: bust the pyramid

What You Do

1 Players "draw" a small circle, about 1 foot across, on the hard floor using the dental floss. Players decide which order to play in and agree on how many rounds to play.

2 The first player builds a pyramid of marbles in the middle of the circle by placing 3 marbles next to each other in a triangle shape and balancing a fourth one on top.

3 The next player shoots his or her taw, or shooter marble, at the base of the pyramid. A taw is usually slighter larger and heavier than the other

marbles. The player gets to keep any marbles that are knocked out of the circle.

4 After the player's turn is over, set up the pyramid for the next person. The player with the most marbles wins.

Shoot 'Em Up

Number of Players: 2 or more
What You Need: dental floss or tape, marbles
Where to Play: on a hard floor
The Point: capture the most marbles

What You Do

1 Players use the dental floss to make a circle on the flat surface. The circle should be about 2 feet wide.

2 Each player puts the same number of marbles into the center of the circle, saving 1 to shoot at the other marbles to knock them out of the circle. This marble is called the taw. Pick the largest or heaviest marbles to be the taw.

3 To shoot the taw, a player holds it outside the circle as shown in the illustration on page 88 and flicks it toward the marbles.

4 Players keep any marbles they knock out of the circle. Players shoot until they don't knock any marbles out, and they leave the taw where it stopped, unless it rolled outside of the circle.

5 If a player hits an opponent's taw, that player gets all the marbles the opponent has collected so far.

6 After all the marbles have been knocked out of the circle, the player with the most marbles wins.

Shuffleboard

What You Do

1 Players agree on or mark off a scoring area at one end of the table. The scoring area should have 4 sections: a 10-point area nearest the edge of the table, a 7-point area further from the edge, a 8-point area even further from the edge, and a 10-point area near the middle of the table.

2 Each player gets 4 coins and lays them at the opposite end of the table.

3 To begin the game, a player slides 1 coin at a time toward the scoring area. Players can bump their own coins, and gain or lose a point depending on how the coin moves, or have a coin knocked off the table. Players keep their own scores.

4 After sliding each of the 4 coins, the first player adds up the points and collects the coins. Each player gets a turn.

5 The player with the most points wins.

PEN & PAPER GAMES

Word play, guessing games, and more.

Act Out

What You Do

1. Players each write a word that names a person or thing (a noun) on a scrap of paper, and then put the papers into the hat. Do this 3 times, so that there are 3 words from each player in the hat.

2. A player starts the game by picking a piece of paper from the hat and acting out that word. Players can't speak, make sounds, or use any objects to help them act out the word.

> **Number of Players:** 3 or more
> **What You Need:** scrap paper, pencils, hat or paper bag
> **Where to Play:** anywhere
> **The Point:** act out or guess word

3. The other players try to guess the word. The player who guesses correctly takes the next turn picking and acting out a word.

4. Play until all the words are used. Players can keep score of how many words each player correctly guessed.

Add On ...

What You Do

1. Each player gets 3 scraps of paper and a pen. Players write a name on 1 scrap, a place on another, and an activity on the third scrap. Pick fun responses, such as "Madonna," "in the refrigerator in the teacher's lounge," and "flossing."

2. Players set out the 3 hats and collect the scraps, putting all of the "names" in a hat, the "places" in another, and the "activities" in the third hat.

> **Number of Players:** 4 or more
> **What You Need:** paper, pens, 3 hats
> **Where to Play:** anywhere
> **The Point:** keep the story going

3. Players take turns blindly picking 1 scrap from each hat and telling a story based on what's written. The next player says, "And then ..." and takes her turn.

4. Play until all the scraps have been used in the story.

A Hit or Miss

What You Do

1. Players will each make 2 grids, using 1 piece of paper per grid. One grid is the Top Secret Map; the other is the Sea Map.

2. Players draw the grids with 10 horizontal and 10 vertical columns. Players label the horizontal columns 1 through 10, and label the vertical columns A through J.

3. Each player draws 4 ships on the Top Secret Map, using these guidelines: 1 ship is made up of 4 grid squares, 1 ship consists of 2 grid squares, and 2 ships are made up of 2 grid squares. The squares must touch, but they can be horizontal, vertical, or diagonal on the grid.

4. Players turn their Top Secret Maps over so the opponent can't see them.

5. The game begins when 1 player launches a rocket to a location on the opponent's grid. For instance, "E, 7" is a location. The Caller marks that location on the Caller's Sea Map. The opponent has to say whether that was a "Hit" or a "Miss."

6. Players take turns launching rockets and tracking the hits and misses. The first player to sink all of the opponent's ships wins.

Bingo

What You Do

1 One player is the Caller. The caller writes a number and letter on each of the Ping-Pong balls, using the following guide: mark 6 balls with a "B" and label them 1 through 6; mark 6 balls with an "I" and label them 7 through 12; mark 6 balls with a "N" and label them 13 through 18; mark 6 balls with a "G" and label them 19 through 24; mark 6 balls with an "O" and label them 25 through 30.

2 In the meantime, the other players make Bingo sheets using a piece of paper (per player, not including the Caller) and a pen. Each sheet needs a grid with 25 squares.

Number of Players: 3 or more

What You Need: 1 piece of paper per player, pens, lots of coins or buttons, 30 Ping-Pong balls, markers, large bowl or basket, candy prizes

Where to Play: in a room

The Point: mark 5 in a row

3 Players then fill in the numbers on their grids by randomly writing in anything from 1 to 6 under "B," 7 to 12 under "I," 13 to 18 under "N," 19 to 24 under "G," and 25 to 30 under "O." Every grid should be unique.

4 The Caller puts the balls in a large bowl and lays the candy prizes beside. To start the game, the Caller announces what prize the winner will get. The Caller then closes both eyes, reaches into the bowl, and pulls out a ball. The Caller calls out the letter and number on the ball, such as "G 21." Any player who has that combination on a grid places a Bingo chip in that square. The Caller sets the used ball aside.

5 After several turns, the player whose grid spells "Bingo" horizontally or diagonally must be the first to yell, "Bingo!" The Caller decides who yelled first, and then checks the player's grid against the used balls.

6 A winner gets the prize and becomes the new Caller. After a winner is announced, players clear their grids and begin a new game. Play until all the prizes have been won.

B6!

BINGO!!

Bogus

What You Do

1 Divide the coins among the players so that players have an equal number of coins. The players should now be silent until the game begins.

2 Players each grab a pen and piece of paper and write down 3 words. Choose words that are commonly used in conversation, or words that you know a player uses often, such as "like" or "cool." Don't pick prepositions (a, an, the). That's too easy.

3 Players turn their papers over, so no one can see what they wrote, and nod to indicate they are ready to play. When everyone is ready, players begin a conversation that will steer the other players toward using their words.

Number of Players: 4 or more
What You Need: 20 or more coins or buttons, 1 pen and piece of paper per player
Where to Play: anywhere
The Point: watch your words

4 Anytime a player hears someone saying "his" word, the player reaches a hand to the speaker and is given a coin. Every player has to join in the conversation.

5 Players are out of the game when they run out of coins. The last player in the game wins.

Call-Out Crosswords

What You Do

1 Each player draws a grid on a piece of paper, using 5 squares across and 5 squares down, for a total of 25 squares.

2 One player starts the game by saying a letter, any letter. (Be sure to use a lot of vowels.) The players each write that letter in any square to try to create words that can be read forward or backwards in the grid (across, down, or diagonally).

3 Players take turns calling out a letter until all the squares of the grids are filled with letters. Then the players take a few minutes to see how many

Number of Players: 2 or more
What You Need: 1 pen and 1 piece of paper per player
Where to Play: anywhere
The Point: earn points for words

words they spelled out, and give themselves 2 points for every 2-letter word, 3 points for every 3-letter word, and so on.

4 The player with the highest score wins.

Catapult

What You Do

1. Players draw circles on several sheets of paper—enough to put the sheets together to cover an area about 3 feet wide and 3 feet long. Players can place cups on the papers and trace around the bases to make perfect circles. Coloring in the circles is optional.

2. Players agree on a Flip line and take turns standing or sitting there and trying to flip their coins onto a circle. For each flip that lands completely in a circle, the player earns a point.

3. At the end of each round, the player with the most points wins.

Number of Players: 3 or more
What You Need: paper, pens, 3 coins per player, cups (optional)
Where to Play: in a room
The Point: flip coins onto circles

Other Ways to Play

Elimination: Players agree to play 5 rounds, and use a pen and mark circles that a coin has landed in. Those circles can't be used again.

Categories

What You Do

1. Players brainstorm 10 categories (types of things), and each player writes these 10 categories down on a piece of paper. Categories can be anything, such as "Colors," "Songs," and "Holidays."

2. To begin the game, 1 player picks a letter of the alphabet and says it aloud.

3. All players have 1 minute to come up with words that begin with that letter and fit in the categories, and write them down. For instance, if the letter is "R," a player could pick the color "Red," the song "Rudolph the Red-Nosed Reindeer," and the holiday "Ramadan."

Number of Players: 2 or more
What You Need: 1 pencil and 1 paper per player, timer
Where to Play: anywhere
The Point: use the right letter

4. Each player gets a turn calling out a letter and having all players try to think of words to put down for each category. No one should repeat a letter that was already used.

5. Working 1 letter at a time, the players take turns reading their responses aloud. For each answer that begins with the correct letter, a player earns 1 point, except when more than 1 player has the same response. In that case, those players get no points for the answer.

Celebrity

What You Do

1 Each player gets 5 scraps of paper. On up to 3 of the scraps each player can write the name of someone famous. On at least 2 of their scraps, each player must write the name of someone not in the room who is personally known by at least 1 other person in the room. The name written down is a Little-Known Celebrity.

2 The players put the names into the hat. One of the players starts the timer. The player draws a name from the hat 1 at a time and has 1 minute to get the rest of the players to guess the names of as many Celebrities as possible. As that player describes the Celebrity, he can't use any names of people or places. The player can't skip any names.

Number of Players: 4 or more
What You Need: scraps of paper, pencils, hat, timer
Where to Play: anywhere
The Point: get players to guess who

3 The player keeps the scraps of paper with the names of Celebrities correctly guessed by the other players. If the player didn't succeed in making the others guess the name, that name remains a mystery and goes back into the hat.

4 Play until all the scraps have been solved. The player with the most scraps of paper wins.

Memory

What You Do

1. One player is the Tester. The Tester collects the 10 objects in the bag. While the other players are looking away, the Tester puts the objects on the floor and covers them with the towel.

2. When everyone is ready, the Tester uncovers the objects and silently counts to 15. The players should look at the objects and memorize what's there. Then the Tester covers the objects with the towel again.

3. The players write down the objects they saw. The Tester decides how much time to give the players.

4. When the time is up, players get 1 point for each object they remembered.

Number of Players: 3 or more
What You Need: 10 objects, a bag to hold the objects, a towel, 1 pen and 1 piece of paper per player
Where to Play: in a room
The Point: test your memory

Other Ways to Play

When?: Give the players more or less time to memorize, to make the game harder or easier.
What?: Give the players more or fewer objects to memorize.
Where?: Give players an extra point for remembering the location of each object. (One point per object.)

No or Yes

What You Do

1 One player is the Talker. The Talker stands on one side of the room. Players line up side-by-side on the other side of the room.

2 Only the Talker can speak. Players can't speak. Players grab 2 pieces of paper each and use the pen to write "No" on one and "Yes" on the other. To answer, players will hold up 1 of these signs.

3 When the players are ready, the Talker starts the game by asking a question and asking the players to answer yes or no. The Talker should stick to things that are clearly yes or no questions. The Talker could ask anything from "Is my birthday in February?" to "Is a Salamander a fish?"

4 When every player has answered, the Talker reveals the answer. For each correct answer a player takes a step toward the Talker.

5 The first player to reach the Talker becomes the new Talker.

Number of Players: 4 or more
What You Need: 2 pieces of paper per player, a pen
Where to Play: in a room
The Point: answer, but don't speak

Number of Players: 3 or more
What You Need: pens, paper, hat
Where to Play: anywhere
The Point: guess what your friends think

Pals

What You Do

1 Every player gets a piece of paper, a scrap of paper, and a pen. On the scrap of paper, each player writes 1 question that any player might answer during the game. Write questions such as, "What's your favorite book?" or "If you were an animal that lived in the sea, what animal would you be?"

2 Players fold up the scraps of paper and put them all in the hat. They then divide into 2 teams.

3 The teams take turn having 1 player draw a scrap from the hat and read it aloud. (Only one team takes a turn at a time.) That player writes down the answer on his paper while his teammates write down the answer they think he will give on their papers.

4 When everyone is ready, the player who drew the scrap asks his teammates to read what they wrote, one at a time. The teammate then reads his answer and gives his team 1 point for every correct answer they had.

5 When all of the questions have been answered, the team with the most points wins.

Paper Chase

Number of Players: 2 or more
What You Need: 1 sheet loose-leaf paper per player, colored pens or pencils (optional)
Where to Play: in a room
The Point: out-fly the competition

What You Do

1 Each player gets a piece of paper and folds it following the illustrations on this page. (See figures 1 through 5.)

2 Players can decorate their planes using pens or pencils. When everyone has made a plane, the players stand side by side on one side of the room.

3 Players take turns launching their planes. Leave the planes where they land, so everyone can see whose went the furthest. Let the winner of the first launch go first next time.

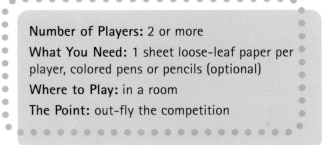

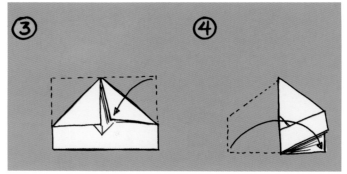

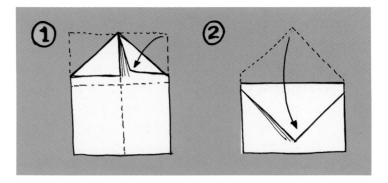

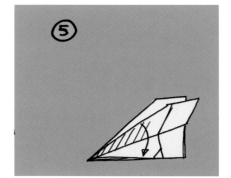

Park It

What You Do

1 Each player gets a piece of paper and takes a turn using the ruler and scissors to cut the paper down to 5 inches wide by 11 inch long.

2 Then the player holds the paper by its 5-inch wide side and cuts a slit lengthwise down the center, all the way to the middle of the paper. See figure 1.

3 The player uses the pencil to mark the edges of the paper right where they line up with the end of the slit he just cut. Then cut a 1 ½-inch slit on each marked edge. See figure 2.

4 The player folds the sides of the paper just below the slits, folding each edge toward the center. The folded sections will overlap. See figure 3.

5 Tape the overlapped sides together. Fold an inch of the bottom edge of the taped side up once.

Number of Players: 2 or more

What You Need: 1 large sheet heavy paper per player, 1 ruler, scissors, 2 paperclips per player, pencil, tape, colored pens or pencils (optional), watch with second hand (optional)

Where to Play: in a room

The Point: be the last pilot to land

See figure 4. Fasten that fold with 2 paper clips. Now fold the top flaps down in opposite directions so the Whirlybird resembles the letter T. See figure 5.

6 Players can decorate their planes using pens or pencils. When everyone has made a Whirlybird, the players stand and, on the count of 3, launch their Whirlybirds by throwing them straight up in the air.

7 As the Whirlybirds drop, their wings flap up and slow the descent. The player whose Whirlybird is the last to touch down wins.

Other Ways to Play

Hang time: Take turns launching each whirlybird and see whose bird floats the longest.

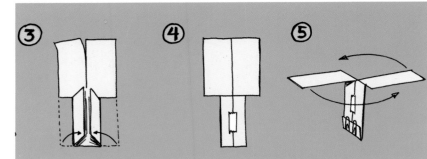

Picture This

What You Do

1. Players divide into 2 teams. Each team needs several pieces of paper and a pen.

2. Each team picks a player to be their first Artist. To choose what to draw, an Artist from either team puts a finger on any page in the book. Both Artists look at the words nearest the finger, without showing anyone else. The nearest noun or verb is what both will draw. (The Artists can tell the players if it is a noun or verb.)

3. The players count aloud together from 1 to 3. After saying, "3," both Artists close their eyes and begin drawing. Artists can't write any words or speak. Teammates try to guess what is being drawn.

4. An Artist tells the team when it's guessed correctly. The first team to figure it out wins.

5. It's fun to look at the drawings again after everyone knows what the Artists were trying to draw. Play several rounds so everyone gets to be an Artist.

> Number of Players: 6 or more
> What You Need: pen, paper, book
> Where to Play: on a table
> The Point: make sense of a blind sketch

Slermcabs

What You Do

1 Each player writes down 5 Slermcabs on a page. (Slermcabs are anagrams, which are words whose letters are scrambled. For instance, "erapp" is an anagram for "paper," "xdime" is an anagram for "mixed," and "slermcabs" is an anagram for "scrambles.")

2 After each player has written down 5 Slermcabs, players swap pages.

Number of Players: 2 or more
What You Need: 1 sheet of paper and 1 pencil per player
Where to Play: on a table or floor
The Point: find hidden words

3 Beginning at the same time, players try to unscramble the words on their pages. The first player to solve all 5 Slermcabs wins.

4 It's okay for a player to solve an anagram by finding a word that's different from what the player who wrote it was thinking.

Super Sketch

What You Do

1 Fold the paper into quarters. Players sketch an original superhero, 1 player at a time. But they can't talk about what they'll draw.

2 As the other players close their eyes, 1 player begins drawing on the uppermost fold of the paper. This player is the Drawer.

3 The Drawer folds the drawn portion down, so it can't be seen, and passes the paper to the next player. Again, everyone except the new Drawer closes both eyes.

4 Players pass the picture until everyone has drawn a section.

5 Players open their eyes, unfold the paper, and see what superhero they created.

Number of Players: up to 4
What You Need: sheet of paper, colored pens or pencils
Where to Play: on a smooth, flat surface
The Point: draw a hilarious picture

Other Ways to Play

What to draw: Agree to draw something else, or agree for each person to draw part of whatever they want. (Players could end up with an alligator head on an airplane's body with cowboy boots on its feet.)

ODDBALLS

Games that are too much fun to classify.

All Thumbs

What You Do

1. Wrap the chocolate bar in wrapping paper. Wrap it several times, so that the bar is completely wrapped at least 3 times. It is the Present. Tape it closed.

2. Players sit in a circle. Put the Present in the middle, along with the oven mitts.

3. To begin the game, players take turns rolling the dice. (One roll per player per round.) If the dice add up to 5, that player quickly puts on the mitts and tries to open the Present.

4. The other players continue rolling the dice as quickly as possible. As soon as another player's

Number of Players: 3 or more
What You Need: chocolate bar, wrapping paper, tape, oven mitts, pair of dice
Where to Play: anywhere
The Point: unwrap the present

roll adds up to 5, the first player must immediately stop trying to open the Present. The next player puts on the mitts and tries.

5. The first player to completely unwrap the Present wins. (If a piece of the chocolate bar breaks off, the player who broke it can eat it after the game ends.)

Avalanche

What You Do

1 One player begins building a mountain of pillows.

2 Whenever the mountain falls, everyone yells, "Avalanche!" and dives into the pillows. Then it's the next player's turn to build.

3 The player who builds the tallest mountain wins.

Number of Players: 2 or more
What You Need: pillows of all sizes
Where to Play: in a room
The Point: build the highest mountain

Beanbag It

What You Do

1 The paper bags are the targets. The players number the targets (1, 2, 3) and arrange them on one side of the room.

2 Players agree on and mark a Throw Line at least 6 feet away from the targets, and then take turns tossing their beanbag into each target in the correct order.

3 The first player to get his beanbag into each target (in order) wins.

How to Make a Beanbag

Make a beanbag out of an old sock and dry beans. Fill the toe of the sock with the dry beans and tie the top of the sock into a knot.

Number of Players: 2 or more
What You Need: 3 paper bags or buckets, string (optional), 1 beanbag per player
Where to Play: on a floor
The Point: score the most points

Bodyguard

What You Do

1 One player is the Bodyguard. The Bodyguard stands in the middle of the room and sets the soda bottle nearby. The soda bottle is the Client. (The Bodyguard can name the Client after some-one famous.)

2 The other players are the Fanatics. They sit in a circle at least 3 feet from the Client and try to roll the ball into it. The Bodyguard tries to protect

Number of Players: 4 or more
What You Need: soda bottle with cap half filled with water, ball
Where to Play: in a room
The Point: protect the Client

the Client by blocking the ball with any body part. The Bodyguard can't touch the Client.

3 Fanatics rebound the ball and re-roll it as quickly as possible. If a Fanatic knocks over the Client, that Fanatic becomes the new Bodyguard.

Capture the Flag

What You Do

1 Players divide into 2 teams, and divide the play area into 2 territories. One team controls each territory, and the more area between the territories, the better. (So, 1 team could have the living room and the other could have a bedroom that's down the hall from the living room.)

2 To begin the game, each team has 1 Flag and hides it. Both teams can send Spies to watch the other team, but both teams can also post lookouts to warn teammates about the Spies.

3 When both teams have hidden their Flags, they announce it and the game begins: each team tries to find and capture the other's Flag and bring it to

Number of Players: 6 or more
What You Need: 2 different flags or 2 different t-shirts
Where to Play: in a house
The Point: steal your opponent's flag

their territory. An opponent tagged in enemy territory must sit in a Jail and can only be freed by the touch of a teammate.

4 The first team to capture the opponent's Flag and take it to their territory wins.

Chef

Number of Players: 3 or more
What You Need: popcorn in a large bowl, timer, bandana, 1 cereal bowl per player, serving spoon
Where to Play: on a table
The Point: spoon the most popcorn

What You Do

1 Set the popcorn on the table and give everyone a cereal bowl.

2 Players take turns standing in front of the popcorn, blindfolded with the bandana, and given the serving spoon. Each player has 1 minute to move popcorn into her cereal bowl.

3 After everyone has had a turn, the player who has the most popcorn in her bowl wins. Eat the popcorn!

Clothespins

What You Do

1. Players agree on a time limit for the game, such as 3 minutes. Use a timer or appoint a Referee who has a watch.

2. Players attach 3 clothespins to the sleeve or bottom of their shirts. When everyone's ready, the players try to steal the clothespins off other players' shirts. Players can move away to keep someone from stealing their clothespins, but players can't push a hand away or protect clothespins.

3. Players can take only 1 clothespin from another player at a time. After a player grabs a clothespin, that player must count out loud to 3 while attaching it to his or her shirt. During this counting, nobody can steal any of that player's clothespins.

4. When time's up, the player with the most clothespins wins.

Number of Players: 4 or more
What You Need: a timer (optional), lots of clothespins
Where to Play: in a room
The Point: keep your clothespins

Number of Players: 4 or more
What You Need: various items, 1 paper bag
Where to Play: anywhere
The Point: identify items by touch

Could Be...

What You Do

1. One player is the Collector and collects various items that are hard to identify by feel alone. (How about a small jar of lip gloss, a single piece of unwrapped candy, or a scoop of ice cream in a plastic bag?) The Collector puts each item into the bag.

2. The players sit in a circle. The Collector hands the bag to a player and the player tries to figure out what is in the bag just by reaching inside and feeling each item. Each player can make 1 guess per turn. If he's correct, he takes the item out of the bag, and then passes the bag to the next player.

3. After all the items are named, the player with the most correct guesses win.

Disc Golf

What You Do

1 Players create a Disc Golf Course in the house. Use trashcans for targets (called "holes"). The Course can go upstairs, downstairs, and all around the house. The more holes and the more distance between each, the better.

2 Each player gets a pencil, a piece of paper, and 1 plate Disc to mark with initials or a doodle. Players stand at Start and take turns making a toss, trying to get their Discs into the hole on the first toss. Any player whose Disc lands in the target on the first toss records a perfect score of 0.

3 Players whose discs don't make it on the first toss must stand where the Disc came to rest and throw from there. Players take turns and let all players finish the round before starting the next round.

4 The score for each player for each round is the total number of tosses made. Players mark their scores and, while still standing near the first target, take turns at the second hole.

5 Once all the holes have been played, the player with the lowest score wins.

Flashlight Tag

What You Do

1 One player is IT. IT decides on the theme, such as "actors" or "books," and tells the players.

2 IT stands in the middle of the room holding the flashlight. IT closes both eyes. The other players spread out in the room, but can't hide behind anything.

3 IT counts aloud from 1 to 3, and after "3" the players begin moving quietly around the room. At any time IT can open both eyes and shine the flashlight on a player. The player must yell the name of an actor (or whatever fits the theme) before the light shines on her head or face. If he's too slow, he's Out of the game.

Number of Players: 5 or more
What You Need: a flashlight
Where to Play: in a dark room
The Point: think fast or be Out

4 If the player survives, IT closes both eyes and the game continues. The last player in the game wins and becomes the new IT.

Hackeysack

What You Do

1 Players take turns bouncing the hackeysack off any body part. Players might use their hands, feet, knees, head, etc., to keep it in the air for as long as possible.

2 A hit is a Hack, and all players count the Hacks aloud. A player's turn ends when the hackeysack hits the floor, a wall, or anything other than the player.

3 After everyone has had a turn, the player who had the most Hacks wins.

Make a Jianzi

A jianzi is a Chinese shuttlecock that you can use like a hackeysack. Make a jianzi with 2 quarters, a large paper napkin, and a little bit of string. Put 2 quarters in the center of the napkin. Fold the edges of the napkin up and twist the napkin tight above the quarters. Use the string to tie a knot there.

Number of Players: 2 or more
What You Need: hackeysack or jianzi
Where to Play: in a room
The Point: get the most Hacks

I Sit ......

What You Do

1. The players put the chairs in wide circle. (There's 1 empty chair.) Players sit down in the chairs and then count out loud together from 1 to 3.

2. After "3," both players on either side of the empty seat try to sit there first. The Loser sits back down, but the Winner looks at any 1 player and says, "I sit..."

3. That 1 player quickly moves to the new empty seat, and says, "in the circle with my friend _____," naming any player.

4. The player named rushes to fill the newest empty seat before the players from either side of it sit there. Whoever gets the chair is the Winner, and the game continues.

Number of Players: 4 or more
What You Need: chairs for each player, plus 1
Where to Play: in a room
The Point: fill the empty seat

Limbo

What You Do

1 Players pick 2 players to hold the Limbo stick (that's the broom handle or long stick). All of the other players line up behind the stick.

2 The Holders each take 1 end of the stick and hold it level, about chest-high. The other players walk under the stick by bending backward. Players can't touch the stick, and only their feet can touch the ground.

3 After each round, the Holders lower the stick. The player who can complete the lowest Limbo wins.

Number of Players: 4 or more
What You Need: broom handle or long stick
Where to Play: anywhere
The Point: see how low you can go

Model

What You Do

1. Players divide into teams with 3 or more players each. One player on each team puts on an extra shirt, dress, or robe. This player on each team is a Model 1. Model 1's clothes should be on correctly, with all buttons buttoned, etc.

2. Model 1 uses 1 hand to hold the hand of a teammate, who becomes Model 2. The remaining players from each team are the Dressers. They must move the extra clothes from their Model 1 to their Model 2. The models must hold hands the whole time.

3. The first team to move the clothing (and re-button all the buttons, etc.) wins.

Number of Players: 6 or more
What You Need: several shirts, dresses, or robes
Where to Play: anywhere
The Point: change clothes

Number of Players: 5 or more
What You Need: a radio, a CD and a CD player, or other music source; chairs for each player, minus 2
Where to Play: in a room
The Point: find a seat when the music stops

Musical Chairs

What You Do

1. One player is the Deejay and controls the music. The other players set out the chairs in wide circle, with 1 chair for each player, minus 1. The Deejay is not counted.

2. To begin the game, the Deejay starts the music. The players walk or dance clockwise around the outside of the circle.

3. The Deejay stops the music at any time, and players scramble to sit down in a chair. The player who doesn't get a chair stands outside the circle. The Deejay starts the music again, and removes a chair. After each music stop, 1 more chair is removed, until there's just 1 chair.

4. The player who sits in the last chair on the last round wins.

Other Ways to Play

Hit the floor: Use paper plates instead of chairs. Players will have to throw themselves down to the floor to secure a spot.

Pick-Up Tug

What You Do

1. Players tie the ends of the rope together to make a circle. Then they lay the rope in the center of the room.

2. Each player grabs 1 tissue and sits on the floor outside of the rope circle, sitting an equal distance from the other players.

3. Each player grips the rope with both hands, and holds the rope tight. The rope should be pulled taut, with no slack. (With 3 players, the rope will be pulled into the shape of a triangle. With 4 players, the rope forms a square.)

4. One at a time, each player is given just enough slack in the rope to use 1 free hand to reach as far back as possible and place a tissue there. The tissue must be out of reach when all the players pull the rope tight again.

> **Number of Players:** 3 or more
> **What You Need:** 8 to 10 feet of rope, 1 tissue per player
> **Where to Play:** in a room
> **The Point:** outpull the opponents

5. When everyone is ready, players tug on the rope and try to reach their tissue. The first player to succeed wins. There can be second- and third-place winners, too.

6. Players can either pull with both hands or use just 1 hand. No one can let go of the rope.

Other Ways to Play

Add players: If there are more than 4 players, add 2 to 3 feet of rope and 1 tissue per extra player.

Sam Squeezer

What You Do

1 Tear off a scrap of paper per player and mark an X on 1. Put the scraps into a hat and have everyone draw 1. Whoever gets the X is Sam Squeezer, but shouldn't tell anyone.

2 The players sit in a circle, memorize who is sitting where, and then grab hold of each other's hands and close their eyes.

3 Sam Squeezer rapidly squeezes 1 or both of the hands she holds, squeezing 1 or more times.

Number of Players: 5 or more
What You Need: scraps of paper, pencil, hat
Where to Play: in a room
The Point: find Sam Squeezer

4 The squeeze will travel that many hands away. So, for each squeeze, the player who receives it deducts 1 squeeze and passes it on. Any player who receives just 1 squeeze is Out. That player moves away and the others tighten the circle and join hands.

5 Players can try win by to guessing who is Sam Squeezer is, but a player who guesses wrong is Out. Sam Squeezer wins by eliminating all the others.

Scavenger Hunt

What You Do

1 A player chosen to be Leader (or an adult) makes a list of items to find in the play area. The descriptions should be creative, such as "something square," "something soft," "something clean," "something green," etc.

2 The Leader gathers the players at a Start location and shows the list to the players. The players copy down the list on a piece of paper. If there are a lot of players, they can work in groups. Otherwise, each player gets 1 list, 1 pencil, and 1 bag.

3 When everyone is ready, players agree on a stop time (10 minutes for an easy game, longer for a game with lots of objects). Then the Hunt begins. Players should move quickly and quietly. When a player finds an item from the list, the player puts it into the bag and marks it off the list.

Number of Players: 5 or more
What You Need: 1 paper, pencil, and bag per player; a timer or watch
Where to Play: in 1 or more rooms
The Point: find the most stuff

4 The Leader calls out when time is up, and all players return to Start and show what they found. The Leader decides whether the objects match the descriptions on the list.

5 The player with the most objects from the list wins.

Shoe Struggle

What You Do

1 Players take off 1 shoe and pile them in the middle of the room. Then they form a circle around the shoes and put their arms around the shoulders of the players to the right and left. The players will resemble a team huddle.

2 The players move clockwise around the shoes while counting out loud together from 1 to 5. After saying "5," everyone tries to get their own shoe back on, without letting go of the shoulders of the other players.

3 The first player to get the right shoe back on wins.

Other Ways to Play

Double trouble: Players put both shoes in the middle.

Smuggler

What You Do

1 One player will be the Smuggler. While the other players are looking away, the Smuggler hides 1 coin in each backpack, and also stuffs each bag full of clothes and other items. The Smuggler zips up or closes the backpacks.

2 The Smuggler then hands 1 backpack to each player and says, "Go." Players immediately search inside for the hidden coin. None of the contents of the backpack can touch the floor—and the backpack can't touch the floor, either.

3 The first player to find the hidden coin without dropping anything wins.

Number of Players: 3 or more
What You Need: 1 backpack, small suitcase, or messenger bag per player, clothes and other items you might take on a trip
Where to Play: in a room
The Point: find the coin

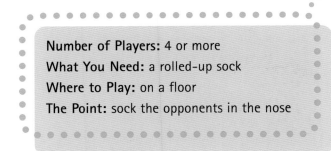

Number of Players: 4 or more
What You Need: a rolled-up sock
Where to Play: on a floor
The Point: sock the opponents in the nose

Sock 'Em

What You Do

1 Players lie down head to head on the floor. If there are a lot of players, their heads will form a circle.

2 One player begins the game by tossing the rolled-up sock into the air, trying to make it land on the nose of an opponent. Aim is important, because it's easy to throw the sock at your own nose by mistake.

3 Players can't move to dodge the sock, they can catch it. Each time a player socks an opponent in the nose, that player earns 1 point. Each time a player catches the sock, that player can toss it and try to earn 1 point.

4 Play until someone earns 4 points.

Other Ways to Play

More parts: Add points for socking other body parts.

Spin Me a Yarn

Number of Players: 5 or more
What You Need: ball of yarn
Where to Play: anywhere
The Point: start and stop on each knot

What You Do

1 Players unravel a length of yarn and tie knots in it at random distances, and then re-roll the yarn into a ball.

2 A player starts the game by holding the yarn, closing both eyes, and telling a story while slowly pulling the yarn between 2 fingers.

3 When the player feels a knot, it's time to pass the yarn to the next player. Even in the middle of a word!

4 Play until the ball of yarn is unraveled.

Spotlight

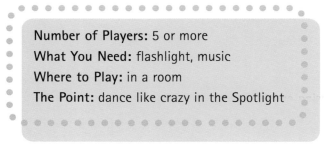

Number of Players: 5 or more
What You Need: flashlight, music
Where to Play: in a room
The Point: dance like crazy in the Spotlight

(SNICKER) (SNICKER)

What You Do

1 One player is IT. IT picks the music and turns it on. Then IT stands in the middle of the room and holds the flashlight.

2 The other players are Dancers. The Dancers form a loose circle around IT and walk or dance around the circle.

3 Whenever IT wants, IT shines the light on a Dancer. The Dancer has 5 seconds to dance and make IT laugh.

4 A Dancer wins by making IT laugh. That Dancer becomes the new IT.

Squares

What You Do

1 Divide the toothpicks among the players. It doesn't matter how many toothpicks you start with. One player sets the timer for 1 minute and says, "Go!"

2 Each player rushes to lay out the toothpicks in square or rectangular patterns. Each player's patterns must work together to create 1 big square or rectangle. No triangle or other shapes allowed.

3 When time's up, all players stop. The player with a completed square or rectangle who also has the most shapes within it wins.

Other Ways to Play

Other shapes: Agree to make the shape of a triangle, using only triangles.

Number of Players: 1 or more
What You Need: a box of toothpicks, timer
Where to Play: on a flat surface
The Point: build a the biggest square

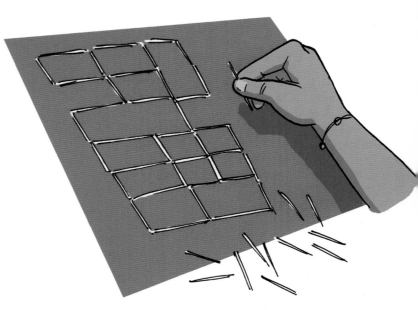

Stomp

Number of Players: 3 or more
What You Need: bubble wrap (it's used to pack fragile items)
Where to Play: in a room
The Point: stomp out all your bubbles

What You Do

1 Each player gets a piece of bubble wrap of similar size. Players count aloud together from 1 to 3. After "3," players stomp as fast as they can to burst all their bubbles.

2 The first player to stomp out all their bubbles wins. Other players can then finish their stomping.

Tidal Wave

Number of Players: 5 or more

What You Need: towels of various sizes (hand towels, bath towels, etc.)

Where to Play: in a room

The Point: reach an Island—quick!

TIDAL WAVE!!!

What You Do

1 Players scatter the towels around the room, laying them on the floor, unfolded. These towels are the Islands. Every other part of the floor is part of the Sea.

2 One player is the Lookout. The other players are the Castaways. To begin the game, the Castaways stand on the Islands without touching each other. The Lookout can stand anywhere. The Lookout says, "The coast is clear." That's the signal for the Castaways to step off the Islands and play in the Sea.

3 The Castaways can pretend to be swimming, diving, or whatever, as long as they are moving around in the Sea. In the meantime, the Lookout removes 1 Island, any Island, because it has been by submerged by an oncoming Tidal Wave.

4 At any time after removing an Island, the Lookout yells, "Tidal wave!" That's the signal for the Castaways to rush back onto an Island. Anyone who doesn't make it in time, and any players who are touching, must stay in the Sea for the rest of the game.

5 Play until there's just 1 Island and 1 remaining Castaway. The winner becomes the new Lookout.

Ultimate Sing-Along

Number of Players: 6 or more
What You Need: flashlight
Where to Play: in a room
The Point: out-sing the competition

What You Do

1. One player is the Emcee. It's best when the Emcee knows all of the players, knows a lot of songs, and likes to act zany. All the other players divide into 2 teams and stand on opposite sides of the room.

2. The Emcee stands in the middle of the room and holds the flashlight.

3. When everyone is in place, the Emcee begins the game by introducing the song to be sung. (The Emcee should pick a popular song that everyone has heard.)

4. The Emcee shines the flashlight on a team. That team starts singing the song. It doesn't matter how it sounds, but the words have to be right. At any time, the Emcee can shine the flashlight on the other team instead. The first team stops singing, and the other team picks up the song.

5. If a team messes up a song or doesn't stop or start on time, they lose a player. The last team still in the game wins.

Under and Over

Number of Players: 4 or more
What You Need: 1 balloon per pair of players
Where to Play: in a room
The Point: send a balloon down and up and up and down

What You Do

1. Players pair up and stand back to back with their elbows linked. If there's an extra player, let that person be the Referee.

2. One player from each pair holds a balloon between both hands.

3. When the game begins, the pairs pass the balloon first between their legs and then over their heads, back into the hands of the first player.

4. The elbows of the teammates must stay linked. The balloon may not touch the floor.

5. The first team to pass the balloon under and over 3 times wins.

Who Am I?

What You Do

1 Players agree on a topic, such as "teachers," "authors," "athletes," "scientists," "book characters," etc. Each player has to be able to think of the name of a person who fits in that topic. (Keep the name a secret for now.)

2 Players find partners. If there's an extra player, there can be 1 group of 3 players. Each player writes the name on a nametag and sticks it on the back of the partner.

3 The game begins when players begin asking questions in order to figure out who they are. The only answers allowed are "Yes" and "No." Players can move among all players to ask questions. (They don't have to stick with their partner.)

4 Play until all players have guessed their identities.

Number of Players: 4 or more
What You Need: name tags, or scraps of paper, pencils, and tape
Where to Play: in a room
The Point: find out who you are

Whose Got It?

Number of Players: 4 or more
What You Need: a shoe
Where to Play: in a room
The Point: find the Thief

What You Do

1 One player sits in the middle of the room. This is the Detective. The other players sit in a circle around the Detective.

2 The Detective takes off 1 shoe, closes both eyes, and begins counting to 10. One of the other players picks up the shoe and begins passing it around the circle. Players pass the shoe behind their backs.

3 On the count of 10, the Detective opens both eyes and must guess who is holding the shoe. It's fun to look hard at each player to see who cracks under the scrutiny and questioning. (Players should not say anything in response to the Detective's questions or comments.)

4 If the Detective correctly guesses who the Thief is, the shoe is returned and the game begins again. If the Detective guesses incorrectly, the Detective closes both eyes again, and play continues.

5 If the Detective guesses wrong 3 times, the Thief holding the shoe becomes the new Detective.

Winks

What You Do

1 Players sit in a circle. One player tears off one scrap of paper per player, and draws a small X on one of the scraps. The player folds up each paper scrap, mixes them up, and puts them into the hat.

2 Players draw 1 paper scrap each, and peek at it. Whoever gets the X is IT and can pass the Sleeper Wink, but must keep it a secret. All players fold up their scraps and put them back into the hat.

Number of Players: 4 or more
What You Need: scrap paper, pencil, and hat
Where to Play: anywhere
The Point: beware the Sleeper Wink

3 To start the game, players look at each other cautiously. At any time IT can make eye contact with a player and wink. A player who is winked at has to close both eyes immediately and slump over. The player is out of the game and can snore loudly or pretend to be dreaming.

4 If anyone sees IT wink, that player shouts "IT!" and names the player in an accusation, such as "Lynn is IT." One other player has to second the accusation. The accused player must tell the truth, and say, "I am IT," or, "I am not IT."

5 If the Accusers are wrong, they are both out of the game. If the Accusers are correct, the game is won.

Wu-Tan

What You Do

1 One player is the Ninja. The rest of the players are Warriors. The Warriors form a circle around the Ninja.

2 The Ninja does an elaborate bow, and then jumps into action. If the Ninja flings either hand open in the direction of the heads or feet of the Warriors, those Warriors must duck or jump to avoid the Ninja's Flying Daggers. If the Ninja motions as if swinging a Blade at the heads or feet of the Warriors, those Warriors must duck or jump to avoid

Number of Players: 4 or more
What You Need: nothing
Where to Play: in a room
The Point: dodge the Ninja's weapons

the Blade. (The Ninja and Warriors can add any sound effects they like.)

3 Any Warrior struck by a combination of Flying Daggers or Blades a total of 3 times is Out. The last Warrior becomes the new Ninja.

Metrics

Need to convert the measurements in this book to metrics? Here's how:

To convert inches to centimeters, multiply by 2.5.

To convert feet to meters, multiply by .3.

Index